Ahmed Fraz Baig

An Improved and Robust Anonymous Authentication Scheme for Roaming in Global Mobility Networks

Anchor Academic
Publishing

Baig, Ahmed Fraz: An Improved and Robust Anonymous Authentication Scheme for Roaming in Global Mobility Networks, Hamburg, Anchor Academic Publishing 2017

Buch-ISBN: 978-3-96067-147-3
PDF-eBook-ISBN: 978-3-96067-647-8
Druck/Herstellung: Anchor Academic Publishing, Hamburg, 2017

Bibliografische Information der Deutschen Nationalbibliothek:
Die Deutsche Nationalbibliothek verzeichnet diese Publikation in der Deutschen Nationalbibliografie; detaillierte bibliografische Daten sind im Internet über http://dnb.d-nb.de abrufbar.

Bibliographical Information of the German National Library:
The German National Library lists this publication in the German National Bibliography. Detailed bibliographic data can be found at: http://dnb.d-nb.de

Hermannstal 119k, 22119 Hamburg
http://www.diplomica-verlag.de, Hamburg 2017
Printed in Germany

Acknowledgments

I am very grateful to *ALLAH* the *ALMIGHTY* for without His grace and blessing this study would not have been possible.

Foremost, I would like to express my sincere gratitude to my supervisor *Dr. Shehzad Ashraf Chaudhry* for the continuous support of my MS study and research, for his patience, motivation, enthusiasm, and immense knowledge. His guidance helped me in all the time of research and writing of this thesis. I could not have imagined having a better advisor and mentor for my MS study.

I would also like to acknowledge my friends, and colleagues. All of them encouraged and provided logistic and technical help during this research.

I would like to admit that I owe all my achievements to my truly, sincere and most loving parents and friends who mean the most to me, and whose prayers have always been a source of determination for me.

Abstract

Global Mobility Networks(GLOMONET) plays very important role in wireless communication. Due to the rapid growth of technology in wireless communication different security challenges have been raised up in GLOMONET. A secure and threat-proof authentication protocol in wireless communication may overcome the security issues because it permits only a legitimate user to access the services. Recently, Karuppiah-Saravanan found Rahee et al's scheme suffers with various attacks and proposed a new scheme by using Diffie-Hellman key agreement protocol, Gope-Hwang pointed out that Wen et al. scheme suffers with many security problems and Islam et al. proposed new authentication Chaotic Maps based scheme. This thesis points out that Karuppiah-Saravanan's scheme is vulnerable to Impersonation attack, Replay attack and key guessing attacks and the Gope-Hwang's scheme cannot resist the replay attacks, Dos attacks and scheme does not verify the user and password locally. Whereas, Islam et al's scheme is failed to accomplish mutual authentication and user anonymity. Thus, this thesis introduced EEC based an improved and robust protocol to overcome all security flaws and to attain computational efficiency in Global Mobility Networks. The security analysis of proposed work is checked formally and informally. Further security and computational analysis reveals that our proposed authentication scheme can withstand all possible attacks in GLOMONET with the features of user anonymity, user friendliness and efficient computation cost.

Contents

List of Figures

List of Tables

Chapter 1

Introduction

The wireless communications are extensively used in current decade, the internet based applications are accessed by mobile networks at anytime and from anywhere. Nowadays, roaming in mobile communication become extremely famous.

Mobility is function that allows a user to move around and inside the network, the network that enables the mobility services to the user is called mobility network and the use of mobility services around the glob is called global mobility networks(GLOMENT). Global Mobility Networks(GLOMONET) plays very important role in wireless communication, it is a commodious domain which enables a roaming user to access their home mobile services in a foreign country. Due to the technological improvements many security issues have been raised up. The security is main issue in wireless communication because, anyone may intercept the communication anytime. While designing the security protocols for wireless network, communication and computation cost is very important. While traveling the roaming service assures that our mobile or wireless devices are connected with a network without any breakage of connection. When a person visits some other country he/she has to use the mobile services. In GLMONET the roamer user at foreign country use the mobile services with the help of their home country network. Mobile User connects themselves to foreign network and Foreign network verifies the legality of mobile user through their home network and Home Agent.

1.1 Authentication in GLOMONET

Authentication is a process that verifies whether someone is in fact who or what it claims to be. There are three types of authentication 1) Single factor-authentication(password based-authentication) 2) Two factor-authentication(smart-card based-authentication) 3) Three/multi-factor authentication in which human body involves(like biometric based-authentication). Authentication of a user is very important in mobility networks. When a mobile user roams in foreign country the authentication ensures that mobile user is a legal user. The valid authentication is required against illegal usage. Many authentication schemes have been proposed for the prevention of illegal usage of mobility services [1-19], Still the schemes are vulnerable under many attacks. Mutual authenticity is a real issue for mobility networks, some schemes [1-3] tried to solve the mutual authentication problem but with respect to time many problems are notified in existing scheme. For the security of Global Mobility Networks some features of security protocol are concerned carefully like: 1) The scheme provide the user friendliness 2) schem provide user anonymity 3) Enable a user to change/update the password anytime 4) scheme does not reveal the location of the user 5) scheme provides forward and backward secrecy 6) prevention of insider attacks 7) Combat against Password guessing attack 8) Capability to withstand replay attacks 9) Capability to withstand the forgery and impersonation attack 10) Capability to achieve the mutual authentication 11) Capability to withstand the man-in-middle attack. Different authentication schemes are proposed to achieve the above listed requirements in the past, some are discussed in below in related works. In this thesis we review some recent schemes like Karuppiah-Saravanan's scheme, Gope-Hwang scheme and Islam et al's and found that these recent schemes are vulnerable to numerous attacks, So this thesis provides a secure authentication scheme for GLOMONET to overcome all security flaws.

1.2 Preliminaries

This section describes the basic background of hash function and ECC.

1.2.1 Hash Function

A function that takes arbitrary sized data as input and converts it to fixed size of data $H : \{0,1\}^* \in Z_p$. The output value is called hash value. Hash function can be defined in following properties:

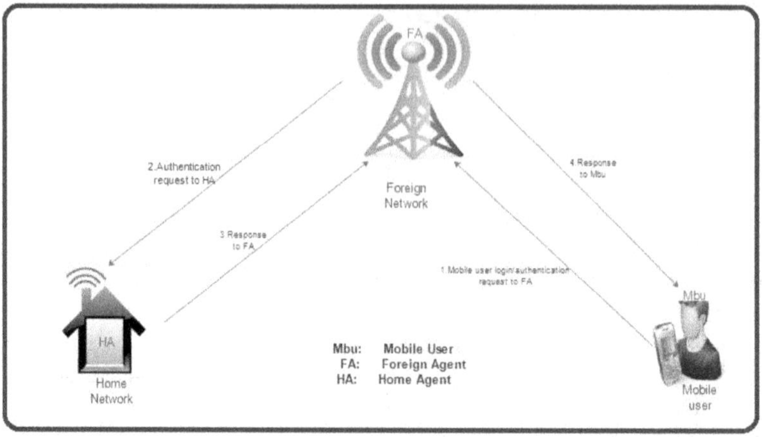

Figure 1.1: Global Mobility Networks Authentication

- Suppose, on any given input value b, the H(b) can be easily computed.
- According to preimage resistance property, on a given value H(b) it's infeasible to compute the value of b.

1.2.2 Elliptic Curve Cryptography(ECC)

A public-key Cryptography that has small key size but provides equivalent security as compared to non-ECC. $y^2 = x^3 + ax + b\text{mod}p$ where a,b belong to finite fields and $(4a^3 + 27b^2 \not\equiv 0)$ the ECC allows scalar point addition P+Q=R and equation can be computed as $(x_p, y_p) + (x_q, y_q) = (x_r, y_r)$ where $x_r = (\lambda^2 - x_p - x_q)$, $y_r = \lambda(x_p - x_r) - y_p$ and $\lambda = \frac{y_q, y_q}{x_q - x_p}$ and point multiplication is defined as $nP = P + P + ..., +P$ with equation $\lambda = \frac{3x_p^2 + a}{x_q - x_p}$. It can be used with Diffie-hellman for key key exchange also with DSA, ECIES and etc.

1.3 Objectives

Objective of this thesis is to propose an authentication scheme that has ability to detect and resist all possible attacks. Formal security analysis and authenticity of proposed thesis is analyzed with BAN logic and ProVerif. Furthermore, we checked the security of proposed scheme informally, against different attacks. Additionally, the scheme offers:

1. Computational efficiency.
2. Communication efficiency.
3. Low latency an delay.

1.4 Thesis outline

Further organization of thesis is as follows:

- Chapter 2, provides the literature survey of previous work, detailed review and crypt-analysis of Karuppiah and Saravanan's scheme, Gope-Hwang's scheme and Islam et al.'s scheme. At the end of chapter 2 we have provided the problem statement of our thesis.
- Chapter 3, provides the proposed solution and their four phases(initialization, registration, login-authentication and password change phase).
- Chapter 4, provides the security analysis, this chapter provides the formal analysis with BAN logic and ProVerif(automated tool) and informal analysis against different security requirements. Furthermore this chapter also provides the performance analysis, we have analyzed the computation cost, running time and its comparison with previous work.
- Finally, we made a conclusion in chapter 5.

Chapter 2

Literature Review

2.1 Literature Survey

Zhu-Ma [1] proposed an authentication scheme. Basic purpose of the scheme is to build a model that provides the mutual authenticity, mutual secret key arrangement, user may authenticate the key implicitly.The proposed scheme uses asymmetric cryptosystem whereas the mobile user does symmetric cryptosystem for encryption and decryption. Lee et at. notified that scheme [1] is incompetent to provide the mutual authentication, likewise forgery attacks and backward secrecy are also possible in existing Zhu and Ma's scheme. Lee et al.[2] proposed a simple and an improved authentication scheme for wireless environment that endured the security weaknesses of scheme [1] efficiently.
In [3] Wei et al. also shown that Zhu-Ma's scheme is unable to provide the user anonymity and they pointed out that the scheme is not secure when any relative information leaks. They proposed an improved scheme that covers the authentication and anonymity weaknesses of previous scheme. Wu et al. [4] reviewed Lee et al's scheme and pointed out that scheme [2] failed to provide the anonymity and backward secrecy, and there are possibilities of off-line attack. Therefor they proposed a smile and efficient scheme that handles the user anonymity, secrecy and off-line attacks. Since, Lee et al.[5] introduced an enhance scheme for privacy protection and the prevention of unauthorized access to the network. Xu-Feng [6] proposed a protocol that handles the security flaws and user anonymity for wireless communication, environment. He et al.[7] shown that Wu et al's scheme failed to provide the anonymity and some attacks like replay and impersonation attacks are possible so, He et al. proposed a new authentication scheme for user which is a strong and lightweight authentication scheme. They introduced a new feature if the smart card reveals any information and password do not

disclose the password the attacker cannot breach the security requirements. Xie et al. also proposed new authentication scheme that contest different properties like user shares session key fairly, user anonymity, user untraceablity, two-factor authentication and the scheme works efficiency as compared to previous schemes. Xu et al. proposed a generic authentication scheme for mobile users that removes the synchronization between home agents and mobile user, the proposed scheme does not require any encryption/decryption or signature operation and author claimed that this scheme is more efficient in communication and computation cost than other similar schemes. Li-Lee [8] reviewed the He et al's scheme and found that scheme may not achieve the anonymity of user and key exchange procedure is not fair so Li et al. proposed a enhanced scheme based on He et al's scheme that fulfills the user anonymity and key exchange agreement, but [9] authors signified that Li et al's scheme is ineffective because of computational cost due to Diffie Hellman, also the scheme [9] does not enable the updation of session key. Das [10] also showed that Li et al's scheme is vulnerable, replay attack is possible. In [11] a new enhanced scheme is introduced that covers the weaknesses of previous work. [11] proposed a scheme that is based on some advantages like: User may choose the the password freely, User anonymity is ensured in this scheme, this ensures the mutual authentication and provides session key agreement securely.

Niu and Li.[12] authors demonstrated that Yoon et al's scheme does not achieve the user anonymity and inequity in key management. they introduced novel authentication scheme that achieves user anonymity, eavesdrop attack is impossible and key distribution agreement is fair in proposed scheme. [13] also found that [12] is insure against insider attack, key distribution in not fair and cannot provide the user anonymity, Li proposed a secure scheme by using ECC and Diffie Hellman which showed lightweight efficiency as compared to previous scheme. Jiang et al.[14] identified He et al's scheme cannot obtain two-factor authentication security, possibilities of insider and replay attack and user cannot change the password. The proposed scheme of Jiang et al. enhances the authentication with privacy preservation. They claimed that their enhanced scheme obtains fully two-factor authentication security with less computation and communication cost. [15] authors found Jiang et al. scheme is vulnerable against replay attack and verifier attack, Then they proposed a new scheme that in which user does not share their secret key. They claimed that their scheme provides best security requirements as compared to previous scheme. Farash et al. [16] proposed a lightweight scheme for key authentication in global mobile networks.

Karuppiah-Saravanan [17] found Rhee et al's scheme failed to achieve the user anonymity, absence of user friendliness, and scheme is vulnerable to reply attack, they proposed a new secure authentication scheme and claimed that the scheme is fully secure. Gope-Hwang [18] notified Qi et al. scheme does not fulfill some security requirements with unfair key

Table 2.1: Notation Guide

Notations	Description
Mb_u	Mobile user
HA	Home agent
FA	Foreign agent
PW_{mbu}	password of mobile user
TS_A	Timestamps generated by entity A
SID	Shadow Identity
SC	Smart Card
PK	Public key home agent
s	Secret key of home agent.
SK	Session key betweenMb_u, FA and HA
HF_k	Pre-shared key between home and foreign agent
r, b	Random numbers of Mb_u
r_{fa}	Random numbers of FA
m, c, e	Random numbers of HA
δTS	Expected time interval for transmission delay
ID_{mbu}	Identity of mobile user
ID_{FA}	Identity of foreign agent
ID_{HA}	Identity of home agents
p, q, n	p and q are prime number and n=p.q
$\oplus$	The XOR operation
$h(.)$	one way hash function
$\|\|$	The concatenation operation
PK	=sP
P	Point over ECC
R_T	Registration time

distribution whereas we notifed that Gope and Hwang scheme suffers with many problems . Islam et al. [19] proposed a new scheme by using Chaotic Maps. In this thesis we have shown that Karuppiah-Saravanan, Gope-Hwang and Islam et al.'s scheme suffer with many security problems. We have provided the detailed review and cryptanalysis of scheme [17], scheme [18] and scheme [19] as in following sections:

2.2 Karuppiah-Saravanan's scheme review

Scheme[17] consists of four phases: initialization phase, registration phase, login and authentication phase, password change phase.

2.2.1 Initialization phase

In initialization phase the home agent takes two prime number p, q and calculates the public key PK_A where $PK_A = g^s modn$ and n gcd and secret key and keeps the (s, p, q) secretly.

2.2.2 Registration Phase

Step 1: The Mobile user Mb_u chooses his identity ID_{mbu} ,password PW_{mbu} and a random number R, random number R is used for the protection of PW_{mbu} .Then Mb_u sends the registration request message $M = \{ID_{mbu}, (R \oplus PW_{mbu})\}$ to the Home Agent HA to server through a secure channel.

Step 2: While receiving the message M the HA calculates the $C_i = h(h(ID_{mbu}) \oplus h(R \oplus PW_{mbu}))$mod n, $K_{mbu} = h(h(ID_{mbu})||(ID_{HA}||(a||TS_{RE}) \oplus h(R \oplus PW_{mbu}))$ Where, T_{RE} is registration time and a is random number chosen by HA and for every user the K_{mbu} must be unique. The HA produces an entry in his database for the Mobile user and stores $(ID_{mbu}, r_{ha}, TS_{RE})$ in encrypted form in his entry. After that the HA customizes the smart card with $(C_i, g, PK_A, n, ID_H, Mb_u, r_{ha}, h(.))$ and provides it to Mobile user Mb_u.

Step 3: When Mobile user Mb_u receives his/her smart card He/she puts random number $\mathcal{R}$ into his/her smart card. Ultimately, smart card holds $\{C_i, g, PK_A, n, ID_H, K_{mbu}, R, h(.)\}$.

2.2.3 Login-Authentication Phase

Suppose mobile user Mb_u is in foreign region under the administration of FA. Now the FA authenticates the Mb_u by the help of Home agent. Authentication phase involves the following step as shown in Figure ??

Step 1: $Mb_u \to FA : M1 = \{A_1, SID, U_1, ID_H A, TS_{mbu}\}$
The Mobile User Mb_u puts his card into card reader by using identity and password, then the smart card calculates $C_i^* = h(h(ID_{mbu}^*) \oplus h(R \oplus PW_{mbu}^*))$ mod n and checks $c_i^* = c_i$ if yes then legality holds otherwise session is terminated. The Smart card chooses a random number m and calculates $A_1 = g^m$ mod n, $A_2 = (PK_A)^m$ mod n, SID $= (ID_{mbu}||A_1)_{A_2}) \oplus h(A_1 \oplus A_2)$, K= $K_{mbu} \oplus h(R \oplus PW_{mbu})$, K=h$(ID_{mbu}||ID_H||X_{mbu}||TS_R)$, $U_1 = h(K||A_2||SID||TS_{mbu})$ Where, TS_{mbu} is time

stamp of mobile user. Ultimately a login request is sent by Mobile user to foreign agent by a message M1=$(A_1, SID, U_1, ID_{HA}, TS_m)$.

Step 2: $FA \rightarrow HA : M2 = \{W_i, ID_{FA}, r_{fa}, TS_{FA}, A_1, SID, U_1, TS_{mbu}\}$

After receiving the message M1 foreign agent FA checks the time freshness comparison $TS_F - TS_m \leq \Delta TS_1$ if the comparison fails, FA does not accept the login request otherwise Foreign Agent choses a random r_{fa} and calculates $W_i = h(K_{HFA}||ID_{FA}||r_{fa}||TS_{FA}||A_1||U_1||SID)$ By using the secret key K_{HFA} that is pre-shared, foreign agent FA sends the M2 to Home agent HA, M2= $\{K_{HFA}||ID_{FA}||r_{fa}||A_1||U_1||SID\}$ Where, M2 is the message.

Step 3: $FA \rightarrow HA : M3 = \{K1, U_2, S_1, TS'_{HA}\}$

When HA receives the message M2, the Home agent HA confirms the whether $TS_{HA} - TS_{FA}\ \Delta TS_2$ if the verification fails, the Home agent does not accept the message M2. When HA obtains the shared key between home agent and foreign agent K_{HFA} then he calculates $W_i^* = (K_{HFA}||ID_{FA}||r_{fa}TS_{FA}||A_1||U_1||SID)$. Now HA checks if $W_i^* = W_i$ then it is ensured that foreign agent is legal. If equality does not hold then session is terminated by HA and computes the $A_2^* = (A_1)^s modn = (PK_A)^m$ mod n, $SID \oplus h(A_1 \oplus A_2^*) = (ID_{mbu}||A_1)_{A_2}$. The Home agent uses A_2^* to reveal the mobile user identity and for decryption of $(ID_{mbu}||A_1)_{A_2}$ the home agent also computes the K^* and U_1^* then compares $U_1^* = U_1$ if comparison is true, authentication is verified otherwise Home agent terminates the session and computes the session key $SK = h(h(ID_{mbu}||K^*)ID_{FA}||r_{fa}||ID_{mbu}||A_1)$, $K1 = SK \oplus (ID_{FA}||r_{fa})$, $U_2 = h(h(ID_{mbu}||K^*)ID_{FA}||r_{fa}||ID_{mbu})$, $S_1 = h(SK||ID_{FA}||r_{fa}||A_1)$ The Home agent sends $M3 = \{K1, U_2, S_1, TS'_{HA}\}$ to Foreign agent FA.

Step 4: $FA \rightarrow Mb_u : M4 = \{U_2, r_{fa}, TS'_{FA}\}$

When FA receives the $M3$, he compares the time stamp difference $TS'_F - TS'_H \leq \Delta TS_2$ if comparison fails then FA does not accept the message otherwise the Foreign agent FA computes the SK(session key between home agent and foreign agent) and S^*1 and checks if $S_1^* = S_1$ Then the legality of home user exists and Home user transmit the message $M4 = \{U_2, r_{fa}, TS'_{FA}\}$ to Mobile user Mb_u. Mobile user receives the message $M4$ and compares the time stamp difference(current time stamp Mb_u)$TS'_{mbu} - TS'_{FA}$(Time stamp of foreign Agent FA) $\leq \Delta TS_1$(Legal time interval). In case of failure in comparison, M4 is rejected by mobile user Mb_u. For the sake verification the mobile user Mb_u computes U_2^* where, $U_2^* = h(h(ID_{mbu}||K)||ID_{FA}||r_{fa}||ID_{mbu})$. Then Mb_u verifies whether $U_2^*? = U_2$. If yes then legality between FA and HA is ensured by the Mb_u and both agreed on computation of session key SK =h$(h(ID_{mbu}||K)||ID_{FA}||r_{fa}ID_{mbu}||A_1)$.

2.2.4 Password Change Phase

The proposed scheme allows the user to update or change their password by following steps:

Step 1: When a mobile user Mb_u with a smart card wants to change or update the password, he/she may do so by adding his previous Identity ID^*_{mbu} and password PW^*_{mbu}.

Step 2: When the smart card receives the password change request, It calculates $C^*_i = h(h(ID^*_m) \oplus h(R \oplus PW^*_{mbu})$ mod n and checks $C^*_i = C_i$ If the values of C^*_i and C_i are equal then it ensures that identity and password are correct and legal user is requesting to change his/her. Then, the smart card requests the user to enter the new password PW_{mnew} that wants to keep where, PW_{mnew} is the new password.

Step 3: The Smart card calculates the $C_{new} = h(h(ID^*_m) \oplus h(R \oplus PW^*_{mnew}))$ mod n and $K^*_m = K(m) \oplus h(R \oplus PW^*_{mbu}) \oplus h(R \oplus PW^*_{mnew})$ which is $= h(ID_{mbu}||ID_{HA}||r_m TS_R) \oplus h(R \oplus PW^*_{mnew})$ where, $\{C_i, K_{mbu}\}$ is replaced with $\{C_{new}, K^*_m\}$ and smart card carries $\{C_{new}, g, PK_a, ID_H, K^*_{mbu}, R, h(.)\}$.

2.2.5 Cryptanalysis and security weaknesses in Karuppiah-Saravanan's Scheme

Scheme [17] is based on Diffie-Hellman key exchange system for sharing the common secret key FH_k by using some key agreement. This section provides cryptanalysis of Karuppiah-Saravanan's scheme. We assume that the Adversary $\mathcal{A}$ has following capabilities:

1. The $\mathcal{A}$ has command over the public channels and the remote server and user communicates with these public channels. The adversary $\mathcal{A}$ can intercept the channel and may modify, insert, block or eavesdrop the messages [20].
2. The adversary $\mathcal{A}$ can acquire the SC for a moment or may purloin the SC and can extract the data that is stored in smart card.

The proposed scheme suffers with following attacks:

2.2.5.1 Vulnerable to Replay and Impersonation Attack

Suppose the adversary $\mathcal{A}$ intercepts the communication channel, captures the message M and time stamps passively, when the session ends Adversary begins with a new session and Adversary $\mathcal{A}$ may creates a new timestamp $\overline{TS_{new'}}$ and will replay0 $\overline{M4}$ where $\overline{M4} =$

$\mathcal{M}b_u$	$\mathcal{F}A$	$\mathcal{H}A$
keys ID^*_{mbu}, PW^*_{mbu} $C^*_i = h(h(ID^*_{mbu}) \oplus h(R \oplus PW^*_{mbu}))$ mod n checks $C^*_i = C_i$ $A_1 = g^m modn$ $A_2 = (PK_a)^m modn$ SID $= (ID_{mbu}\|\|A_1)_{A_2} \oplus h(A_1 \oplus A_2)$ K$= K_{mbu} \oplus h(R \oplus PW_{mbu})$ $U_1 = h(K\|\|A_2\|\|SID\|\|TS_{mbu})$		
$\xrightarrow{M1=\{A_1,SID,U_1,ID_{HA},TS_{mbu}\}}$		
	$TS_F - TS_m \leq \triangle TS_1$ select r_{fa} $W_i = h(K_{HFa}\|\|ID_{FA}\|\|r_{fa}\|\|TS_{fa}\|\|A_1\|\|U_1\|\|SID)$	
	$\xrightarrow{M2=\{W_i,ID_{FHA},r_{fa},TS_{FA},A_1,SID,U_1,TS_m\}}$	
		$TS_{HA} - TS_{FA} \leq \triangle TS_2$ $W^*_i = h(K_{HFa}\|\|ID_F\|\|r_{fa}\|\|TS_{FA}\|\|A_1\|\|U_1\|\|SID)$ and checks $W^*_i = W_i$ $A^*_2 = (A_1)^s$ mod n which is equal to $(PK_a)^m)$ $SID \oplus h(A_1 \oplus A^*_2) = (ID_{mbu}\|\|A1)_{A_2})$ Decrypt $(ID_{mbu}\|\|A_1)_{A_2})$ retrieve $\{r_m\|\|TS_R\}$ $K^* = h(ID_{mbu}\|\|ID_{HA}\|\|r_{mbu}\|\|TS_R)$ $U^*_1 = h(K\|\|A^*_2\|\|SID\|\|TS_{mbu})$ checks $U^*_1 =$ U1 $SK = h(h(ID_{mbu}\|\|K^*)\|\|ID_{FA}\|\|r_{fa}\|\|ID_{mbu}\|\|A_1)$ K1 $= SK \oplus h(K_{HFA}\|\|r_{fa})$ $U_2 = h(h(ID_{mbu}\|\|K^*)\|\|ID_{FA}\|\|r_{fa}\|\|ID_{mbu})$ $S_2 = h(SK\|\|ID_{FA}\|\|r_{fa}\|\|A_1)$
		$\xleftarrow{M3=\{K,U_2,S_2,TS'_{HA}\}}$
	$TS'_{FA} - TS'_{HA} \leq \triangle TS_2$ $SK = K1 \oplus h(K_{HFA}\|\|r_{fa})$ $S^*_2 = h(SK\|\|ID_{FA}\|\|r_{fa}\|\|A_1)$ checks $S^*_2 = S_2$	
	$\xleftarrow{M4=\{U_2,r_{fa},TS_F\}}$	
$TS'_{HA} - TS'_{FA} \leq \triangle TS_1$ $U^*_2 = h(h(ID_{mbu}\|\|K)\|\|ID_{FA}\|\|r_{fa}\|\|ID_{mbu})$ checks $U^*_2 = U_2$ $SK = h(h(ID_{mbu}\|\|K)\|\|ID_{FA}\|\|r_{fa}\|\|ID_{mbu}\|\|A_1)$		

Figure 2.1: Karuppiah-Saravanan's Scheme

$\{U_2, r_{fa}, \overline{TS_{new}}\}$ While tracking the message $\overline{M4}$ adversary $\mathcal{A}$ can create $\overline{TS_{new}}$ and random number $\overline{r_{fa}}$. The Adversary $\mathcal{A}$ can also perform the impersonation attack. Although the Adversary $\mathcal{A}$ cannot compute the session key but he may impersonate the mobile user Mb_u to believe that the Adversary $\mathcal{A}$ is a legal Foreign Agent FA.

2.2.5.2 Guessing the secret key of Home agent

As we know that all messages are transmitted through an insecure channel so, Adversary $\mathcal{A}$ may intercept the channel. Suppose the Adversary $\mathcal{A}$ intercepted the channel as $M4 = \{U_2, r_{fa}, TS_F\}$
Now the Adversary $\mathcal{A}$ can guess the Mb_u's secret authentication parameters and even can get ID_{mbu} as Adversary $\mathcal{A}$ knows the public parameters ID_F, r_{fa} he will give a guessing value k_G repeatedly until does not compute U_{2G} where, $U_{2G} = h(h(ID_{mbu}||K_G)||ID_F||r_{fa}||ID_{mbu})$ and Adversary $\mathcal{A}$ will compare $U_2 ?= U_{2G}$ if the guessed value does not match then the Adversary $\mathcal{A}$ will guess another K_G and so on. Guessing a value can be done in polynomial time. When adversary will find the K_2G it can also disclose the Mb_u identity to the adversary.

2.3 Gope-Hwang's scheme review

Gope-Hwang [18] notified that Wen et al. scheme is defenseless form many forgery attacks, their key exchange system in unfair and invites some guessing attacks. They proposed new authentication scheme which carries 3 phases: registration-reestablishment phase, key-agreement with mutual-authentication, and password change phase.

2.3.1 Registration-reestablishment Phase

Registration phase of proposed scheme consists of two steps. Firstly, Mb_u identity to HA for registration.

Step 1: $M : Mb_u \rightarrow HA : \{ID_{mbu}, SID_{mbu}\}$
Mb_u transmits M1 by a secure channel to HA.

Step 2: $M : HA \rightarrow Mb_u : \{SID, K_{mbu}, T_{SN}\}$
When HA receives registration request he/she chooses N_{ha} and r_{ha} random numbers and calculates $K_{mbu} = h(ID_{mbu}||N_{ha})$,m=m+1 and $SID_{mbu} = h(ID_{mbu}||r_{ha}||K_{mbu}||T_{SN})$. The HA customizes the SC with $\{ID_{mbu}, K_{mbu}, T_{SN}, h(.)\}$ and transmits to Mb_u on

secure medium. The mobile user Mb_u calculates the $K^*_{mbu} = K_{mbu} \oplus h(ID_{mbu}||PW_{mbu})$, $SID^*_{mbu} = SID_{mbu} \oplus h(ID_{mbu}||PW_{mbu})$ Afterward he/she exchanges K_{mbu} and SID_{mbu} with K^*_{mbu} and SID^*_{mbu}. Note that SID_{mbu} is sent only for reestablishment.

2.3.2 Mutual-Authentication Phase with key-agreement phase

We suppose that the Mb_u is roaming in foreign country under the administration of foreign networks. To leverage the services of mobile network at foreign country the Mobile user Mb_u has to authenticate himself/herself by the help of Home Agent HA and foreign agent FA. By using the Identity ID and password PW the Mobile User Mb_u authenticates himself/herself and smart card executes the following steps:

Step 1: $M1 = \{V1, ID_{HA}, T_{SNm}\}$. In first step the mobile user Mb_u uses his/her identity ID_{mbu} and PW_{mbu} for login. SC calculates $K_{mbu} = K^*_{mbu} \oplus (ID_{mbu}||PW_{mbu})$. Aftermath N_{mbu} random number is generated and $V1 = (ID_{mbu}||K_{mbu}||n_{mbu}||ID_{FA}||T_{SNm})^2 modn$ is derived and login message M1 is transmitted to FA.

Step 2: $M2 = \{(M1, ID_{FA}, n_{fa}, r_{fa})_{FH_K}, V2\}$
When FA receives M1 he/she chooses randomly n_{fa}, r_{fa} and calculates V2:

$$V2 = \{M1||N_{fa}||N_{fa}||r_{fa}||FH_K\}$$

Afterward foreign agent FA forwards M2 to home agent HA.

Step 3: $M3 = \{V3, V4, n_{ha}, r_{ha}, V5\}$
When HA receives the M2, he/she verifies T_{SNm} if it is true and legal then $h(N_{fa}, r_{fa})_{FH_K}$ is decrypted. Afterward checks $V2? = (M1||n_{fa}||r_{fa}||FH_K)$ if true then gets $\{ID_{mbu}, K_{mbu}, T_{SN}$ Further more following values are computed by HA $Sk = h(h(ID_{mbu}||x)||ID_{FA}||N_{mbu})$, $V3 = (SK \oplus FH_K||N_{fa}||r_{fa})$, $V4 = (V3||FH_K||N_{fa}||r_{fa})$, $n_x = h(ID_{mbu}||K_{mbu}) \oplus N_{fa}$, $T_{SNm} = m$, $n_{ha} = h(ID_{mbu}||T_{SNm}||K_{mbu}) \oplus T_{SNm}$, $V5 = (N_{ha}||r_{ha}||K_{mbu})$ after the computation of all values the message M3 is sent to foreign agent FA.

Step 4: $M4 = \{N_{ha}, r_{ha}, V5\}$
When FA receives the M3 he/she verifies whether $V4? = (V3||FH_K||n_{fa}||r_{fa})$ if valid then session key is computed by system whereas, $SK = (V3 \oplus FH_K||R_{fa}||n_{fa})$ and M4 is transmitted to Mb_u.
When the mobile user Mb_u obtains M4 he/she checks if $V5 \stackrel{?}{=} (N_{ha}||r_{ha}||K_{mbu})$ if validity exist then Mb_u computes $T_{SNmN} = h(ID_{mbu}||T_{SNm}||K_{mbu}) \oplus N_{fa}$, $N_{fa} = h(ID_{mbu}|K_{mbu}) \oplus r_{fa}$, $Sk^* = h(h(ID_{mbu}||K_{mbu}||x||ID_{FA}||N_{mbu})) \oplus N_{fa}$. Where, SK is

session-key and the mobile user Mb_u updates T_{SNm} with T_{SNmN} for further communication.

2.3.3 Password Change Phase

The proposed scheme enables the user to change his/her password by inserting his/her card into the device and the Mb_u enters old identity and password. Then smart card requests the user to enter new password PW^*_{mbu}. Aftermath the SC obtains $K_{mbu} = K^*_{mbu} \oplus h(ID_{mbu}||PW_{mbu})$, $SID_{mbu} = SID^*_{mbu} \oplus h(ID_{mbu}||PW_{mbu})$ and computes $K^{**}_{mbu} = K_{mbu} \oplus h(ID_{mbu}||PW^*_{mbu})$, $SID^{**}_{mbu} = SID_{mbu} \oplus h(ID_{mbu}||PW^*_{mbu})$ At the end SID^*_{mbu} is exchanged with SID^{**}_{mbu} and K^*_{mbu} is exchanged by K^{**}_{mbu}.

2.3.4 Security weaknesses in Gope-Hwang's Scheme

In this section shows that Gope-Hwang's scheme [18] suffers replay attacks, DoS attack and unfair local user verification in login phase which leads to impersonation attacks details of these attacks are as following:

2.3.4.1 Replay attacks

In Gope-Hwang's scheme [18] an adversary $\mathcal{A}$ will intercept the channel and will obtain login-request message $M1 = \{V1, ID_{HA}, Ts_{NM}\}$. As no timestamp is associated with login message $M1$ the Adversary $\mathcal{A}$ can replay M1 in login phase latter on. Likewise the adversary $\mathcal{A}$ will perform the replay attacks in step2 with $M2 = \{(M1, ID_{FA}, n_{fa}, r_{fa})_{FH_K}, V2\}$, in step3 with $M3 = \{V3, V4, n_{ha}, r_{ha}, V5\}$ and in step4 with $M4 = \{N_{ha}, r_{ha}, V5\}$ of authentication phase because no timestamp is used with any message.In fact the adversary $\mathcal{A}$ is unable to compute the session key but adversary will send too many login-authentication request intentionally to overwhelm the Mb_u,FA and HA [21].

2.3.4.2 DoS attacks

As showed in previous section simultaneous repetition of replay attacks in large numbers can exhaust the communication and computation cost and also leads to DoS attacks that may cause the prevention of access the resource to legal user.

2.3.4.3 Impersonation attack and unfair local user verification in login phase

Gope-Hwang's scheme does not provide the local verification of user in login phase as Mb_u computes $K_{mbu} = K^*_{mbu} \oplus (ID_{mbu}||PW_{mbu})$ but there is no comparison whether K_{mbu} is same as is stored in registration phase or not. The adversary $\mathcal{A}$ can register himself/herself as a legal user and after the new session login with $\overline{ID_{mbu}}$ and $\overline{PW_{mbu}}$ afterward computes $\overline{K_{mbu}}$ although the computed $\overline{K_{mbu}}$ is wrong but due to no verification of a user in proposed scheme the adversary $\mathcal{A}$ can go to next values without any comparison and computes $\overline{V1}$ and may impersonate the FA by sending the $M1 = \{\overline{V1}, ID_{HA}, T_{SNm}\}$.

$\mathcal{M}b_u$	$\mathcal{FA}$	$\mathcal{HA}$
Generate n_{mbu} $K_mbu = K^*_{mbu} \oplus (ID_{mbu}\|\|PW_{mbu})$ $V1 = (ID_{mbu}\|\|K_{mbu}\|\|n_{mbu}\|\|ID_{FA}\|\|T_{SNm})^2 mod n$		
$\xrightarrow{M1=\{V1, ID_{HA}, T_{SNm}\}}$		
	Select n_{fa}, r_{fa} $V2 = \{M1\|\|n_{fa}\|\|r_{fa}\|\|FH_K\}$	
	$\xrightarrow{M2=\{(M1, ID_{FA}, n_{fa}, r_{fa})_{FHk}, V2\}}$	
		Verify T_{SNm} Decrypt $h(n_{fa}, r_{fa})_{FH_K}$ $V2 \stackrel{?}{=} \{M1\|\|n_{fa}\|\|r_{fa}\|\|FH_K\}$ Get ID_{mbu}, n_{mbu} $SK = h(h(ID_{mbu}\|\|x)\|\|ID_{FA}\|\|N_{mbu})$ $V3 = (SK \oplus FH_K\|\|n_{fa}\|\|r_{fa})$ $V4 = (V3\|\|FH_K\|\|n_{fa}\|\|r_{fa})$ $n_x = h(ID_{mbu}\|\|K_{mbu}) \oplus n_{fa}$ $m = m + 1$ $T_{SNm} = m$ $n_{ha} = h(ID_{mbu}\|\|T_{SNm}\|\|K_{mbu}) \oplus T_{SNm}$ $V5 = (N_{ha}\|\|r_{ha}\|\|K_{mbu})$
	$\xleftarrow{M3=\{V3, V4, n_{ha}, r_{ha}, V5\}}$	
	$V4^* = (V3\|\|FH_K\|\|N_{fa}\|\|r_{fa})$ $SK = (V3 \oplus FH_K\|\|R_{fa}\|\|N_{fa})$	
	$\xleftarrow{M4=\{n_x, n_{ha}, V5\}}$	
$V^*5 \stackrel{?}{=} (N_{ha}\|\|r_{ha}\|\|K_{mbu})$ $T_{SNmn} = h(ID_{mbu}\|\|T_{SNm}\|\|K_{mbu}) \oplus n_{fa}$ $n_{fa} = h(ID_{mbu}\|K_{mbu}) \oplus r_{fa}$ $SK^* = h(h(ID_{mbu}\|\|K_{mbu}\|\|x\|\|ID_{FA}\|\|N_{mbu})) \oplus N_{fa}$ Update $T_{SNm} = T_{SNmn}$		

Figure 2.2: Gope-Hwang's proposed scheme

2.4 Islam et al.'s scheme review

Islam et al's [19] proposed new authentication scheme which carries 5 phases: registration, Login, authentication, password-change phase and Revocation of lost SC and detailed review of each phase is discussed below:

2.4.1 Registration Phase

Registration phase executes following five steps:

Step 1: The Mb_u chooses ID_{mbu} and password PW_{mbu} freely.

Step 2: Mb_u Transmits registration request along with his/her identity ID_{mbu} to HA.

Step 3: Firstly HA checks the legality if ID_{mbu} afterward SC_{mbu} is chosen. The home agent HA calculates $A_{mbu} = h(ID_{mbu}||SC_{mbu}||S_{ha})$ and stores $(A_{mbu}, p, h(.), PK_{ha})$ into SC and sends to Mb_u.

Step 4: When Mb_u receives SC he/she computes $B_{mbu} = h(ID_{mbu}||PW_{mbu})$,$C_{mbu} = A_{mbu} \oplus B_{mbu}$ and $D_{mbu} = H(A_{mbu}||B_{mbu})$. The SC includes $< C_{mbu}, D_{mbu} >$ into memory and discard $< A_{mbu}, B_{mbu} >$ from the memory.

Step 5: Finally, SC carries $(C_{mbu}, D_{mbu}, p, h(.), x, PK_{ha})$.

2.4.2 Login Phase

Step 1: For login phase Mb_u inserts his/her SC into device and use ID_{mbu} and PW_{mbu}.

Step 2: SC locally verifies $B_{mbu} = h(ID_{mbu}||PW_{mbu})$,$A_{mbu} = C_{mbu} \oplus B_{mbu}$ and $D^*_{mbu} = H(A_{mbu}||B_{mbu})$ if verification becomes true then next step is performed.

Step 3: A timestamp TS_{mbu} and random number r_{mbu} generated by SC. Afterward SC computes $R_{mbu} = Th(r_{mbu}||A_{mbu})S_{HA}(x)$, $DI_{mbu} = Th(r_{mbu}||A_{mbu})PK_{ha}modp$ and $G_{mbu} = h(ID_{mbu}||R_{mbu}||TS_{mbu}||A_{mbu})$

Step 3: Afterward $M1 = \{ID_{FA}, DI_{mbu}, R_{mbu}, TS_{mbu}, G_{mbu}\}$ login message is forwarded to HA.

2.4.3 Authentication Phase

Step 1: In authentication phase when FA receives M1 he/she checks the timestamp comparison if comparison fails then session is aborted. HA calculates $FA_{key} = T.S_{FA}(PK_{ha})$ and $G_{fa} = (ID_{FA}||TS_{FA}||M1||FA_{key})$. Afterward $M2 = \{ID_{FA}, TS_{FA}, M1, FA_{key}\}$ is sent to HA.

Step 2: When HA receives the message he/she verifies the timestamp difference if TS is valid then next step is proceeded and HA computes $FA_{key} = T.S_{FA}(PK_{ha})$, $G^*_{fa} \stackrel{?}{=} (ID_{FA}||TS_{FA}||M1||FA_{key})$ if yes then next step is performed and HA calculates$ID_{mbu} = DI_{mbu} \oplus h(T_x S_{ha}||R_{mbu}) mod p$ to extract the ID_{mbu} and $A_{mbu} = h(ID_{mbu}||ID_{HA}||SC_{mbu}||S_{ha})$ checks $G^*_{mbu} \stackrel{?}{=} h(ID_{mbu}||R_{mbu}||TS_{mbu}||A_{mbu})$ at last HA calculates $G_{HA} = (ID_{FA}||TS_{FA}||M2 ||FA_{key})$ and transmits $M3 = \{ID_{FA}, TS_{HA}, G_{HA}\}$ to FA.

Step 3: When FA receives the message he/she verifies the timestamp difference if TS is valid then it checks whether $G^*_{HA} \stackrel{?}{=} G_{HA}$ if no then session is aborted. FA chooses R_{fa} and computes $SK_{FA} = h(ID_{mbu}||ID_{FA}||R_{mbu}||r_{fa}||Tr_{fa}(R_{mbu}))$ $= h(ID_{mbu}||ID_{FA}||R_{mbu}||r_{fa}||T_{h(R_{mbu}||A_{mbu})}r_{fa}(x))$, $G_{MFA} = (ID_{FA}||r_{fa}||TS_{HF}||SK_{FA})$. Afterward $M4 = \{ID_{FA}, r_{fa}, TS_{HF}, SK_{FA}\}$ to Mb_u.

Step 4: When FA receives the message he/she verifies the timestamp difference if TS if TS interval becomes false then session is terminated otherwise Mb_u computes $SK_{mbu} = h(ID_{mbu}||ID_{FA}||R_{mbu}||r_{fa}||T_{A_{mbu}R_{mbu}}(R_{FA}) = h(ID_{mbu}||ID_{FA}||R_{mbu}||r_{fa}||T_{h(R_{mbu}||A_{mbu})}r_{fa}(x))$ and $G^*_{MFA} \stackrel{?}{=} (ID_{FA}||r_{fa}||TS_{HF}||SK_{mbu})$ if yes then FA is authenticated and SK_{mbu} is accepted.

2.4.4 Password Change Phase

Step 1: To change the password Mb_u will login with with ID_{mbu} and PW_{mbu}.

Step 2: When SC receives the request it computes $B_{mbu} = h(ID_{mbu}||PW_{mbu})$,$A_{mbu} = C_{mbu} \oplus B_{mbu}$ and $D^*_{mbu} = H(A_{mbu}||B_{mbu})$. If $D^*_{mbu} = D_{mbu}$ then Mb_u is requested to enter new PW_{mbu} otherwise session is aborted.

Step 3: Mb_u enters new password PW^*mbu and SC performs following tasks $B^*_{mbu} = h(ID_{mbu}||PW^*_{mbu})$, $C^*_{mbu} = A_{mbu} \oplus B^*_{mbu}$ and $D^*_{mbu} = H(A_{mbu}||B^*_{mbu})$.

Step 4: In last step the SC exchange $< C_{mbu}, D_{mbu}, p, h(.), x, PK_{ha} >$ with $< C^*_{mbu}, D^*_{mbu}, p, h(.) , x, PK_{ha}) >$.

2.4.5 Revocation of lost SC Phase

Step 1: A lost SC request with ID_{mbu} is sent by Mb_u to HA.

Step 2: HA confirms the validity of ID_{mbu} afterward HA computes $A^{**}_{mbu} = h(ID_{mbu}||ID_{HA}||SC^{**}_{mbu}||$ and stores it to SC.

Step 3: New SC is issued to Mb_u

Step 4: The mobile user Mb_u selects new PW^{**}_{mbu} and stores his/her identity ID_{mbu} and PW^{**}_{mbu} in SC.

Step 5: SC Computes $B^{**}_{mbu} = h(ID_{mbu}||PW^{**}_{mbu})$, $C^{**}_{mbu} = A^{**}_{mbu} \oplus B^{**}_{mbu}$ and $D^{**}_{mbu} = H(A^{**}_{mbu}||B^{**}_{mbu})$

Step 6: In last step $< A^{**}_{mbu}, B^{**}_{mbu} >$ are discarded and $< C^{**}, D^{**} >$ are saved in SC.

$\mathcal{M}b_u$	$\mathcal{FA}$	$\mathcal{HA}$
Use $< ID_{mbu}, PW_{mbu} >$ $B_{mbu} = h(ID_{mbu}\|\|PW_{mbu})$ $A_{mbu} = C_{mbu} \oplus B_{mbu}$ $D^*_{mbu} = H(A_{mbu}\|\|B_{mbu})$ $D^*_{mbu} \stackrel{?}{=} D_{mbu}$ choose $TS_{mbu}, R_{mbu} \in Z_p^*$ $R_{mbu} = Th(r_{mbu}\|\|A_{mbu})S_{HA}(x)$ $DI_{mbu} = Th(r_{mbu}\|\|A_{mbu})PK_{ha} mod p$ $G_{mbu} = h(ID_{mbu}\|\|R_{mbu}\|\|TS_{mbu}\|\|A_{mbu})$		
$\xrightarrow{M1=\{ID_{FA}, DI_{mbu}, R_{mbu}, TS_{mbu}, G_{mbu}\}}$		
	check $(TS_{FA} - TS_{mbu})$ is valid? $FA_{key} = T.S_{FA}(PK_{ha})$ $G_{fa} = (ID_{FA}\|\|TS_{FA}\|\|M1\|\|FA_{key})$	
	$\xrightarrow{M2=\{ID_{FA}, TS_{FA}, M1, FA_{key}\}}$	
		check $(TS_{FA} - TS_{mbu})$ is valid? $FA_{key} = T.S_{FA}(PK_{ha})$ $G^*_{fa} \stackrel{?}{=} (ID_{FA}\|\|TS_{FA}\|\|M1\|\|FA_{key})$ $ID_{mbu} = DI_{mbu} \oplus h(T_{xS_{ha}\|\|R_{mbu}}) mod p$ Retrieve $< ID_{mbu}, SC_{mbu} >$ $A_{mbu} = h(ID_{mbu}\|\|ID_{HA}\|\|SC_{mbu}\|\|S_{ha})$ $G^*_{mbu} \stackrel{?}{=} h(ID_{mbu}\|\|R_{mbu}\|\|TS_{mbu}\|\|A_{mbu})$ $G_{HA} = (ID_{FA}\|\|TS_{FA}\|\|M2\|\|FA_{key})$
	$\xleftarrow{M3=\{ID_{FA}, TS_{HA}, G_{HA}\}}$	
	check$(TS_{HF} - TS_{HA})$ is valid? $G^*_{HA} = (ID_{FA}\|\|TS_{FA}\|\|M2\|\|FA_{key})$ $G^*_{HA} \stackrel{?}{=} G_{HA}$ choose $r_{fa} \in Z_p^*$ $R_{fa} = T_{r_{fa}}(x) mod p$ $SK_{FA} = h(ID_{mbu}\|\|ID_{FA}\|\|R_{mbu}\|\|r_{fa}\|\|Tr_{fa}(R_{mbu}))$ $G_{MFA} = (ID_{FA}\|\|r_{fa}\|\|TS_{HF}\|\|SK_{FA})$	
$\xleftarrow{M4=\{ID_{FA}, r_{fa}, TS_{HF}, SK_{FA}\}}$		
check$(TS_{MF} - TS_{HF})$ is valid? $SK_{mbu} = h(ID_{mbu}\|\|ID_{FA}\|\|R_{mbu}\|\|r_{fa}\|\|T_{A_{mbu}R_{mbu}}(R_{FA}))$ $G^*_{MFA} \stackrel{?}{=} (ID_{FA}\|\|r_{fa}\|\|TS_{HF}\|\|SK_{mbu})$ if yes then authenticate FA.		

Figure 2.3: Islam et al. scheme

2.4.6 Cryptanalysis of Islam et al's. scheme

This section shows that Islam et al's. [19] scheme is unable to provide mutual authentication and user anonymity further detailed discussion is as followed:

2.4.6.1 User Anonymity

In Proposed scheme FA used the ID_{mbu} without calculation of $ID_{mbu} = DI_{mbu} \oplus h(T_{xS_{ha}||R_{mbu}}) mod p$ whereas is impossible to get ID without computing DI_{mbu} so this scheme is not a valid scheme. Also auther violated the law of anonymity because FA can see the ID_{mbu} where, FA should not be able to see the ID_{mbu}[12] [17].

2.4.6.2 Mutual Authentication

Islam et al's. scheme is failed to achieve the mutual authentication as $SK_{FA} = h(ID_{mbu} || ID_{FA} || R_{mbu} || r_{fa} || Tr_{fa}(R_{mbu}))$ we know that SK is computed by FA. Session key is not computed by HA also there is no contribution of Home agent HA in computation of session key which is against the law of mutual authentication.

2.5 Problem Statement

In past, simple Symmetric Encryption techniques were proposed for Global Mobility Networks. But the conventional Encryption schemes cannot provide the user anonymity, Whereas the Asymmetric (RSA,Diffie-Hellman) based encryption schemes were proposed to overcome the user anonymity problem.

Some schemes based on public key encryption successfully achieved the user anonymity problem but, with the high computation and communication cost. Recently, in [17] authors found that Rhee et al.'s scheme is vulnerable to many attacks and proposed a new scheme by using Diffie-Hellman key agreement protocol and in [18] Gope-Hwang notified the Wen et al. and Qi et al. suffer with many attacks proposed a new and enhanced scheme for authentication. We found that Karuppiah-Saravanan's scheme [17] is vulnerable to:

1. Impersonation attack.

2. Replay attack.

3. Adversary $\mathcal{A}$ can guess the secret key of Home agent.

Gope-Hwang scheme [18] is vulnerable to:

1. Replay and DoS attacks.

2. Impersonation attack and unfair local user verification

S.K.H Islam et al's. scheme [19] does not achieve:

1. User Anonymity

2. Mutual Authentication

Therefore an improved and robust anonymous authentication scheme for roaming in Global Mobility Networks is needed, to overcome the flaws found in the aforementioned scheme.

2.6 Chapter Summary

This chapter first section discusses the literature review, second section discusses brief reviews and cryptanalysis of Karuppiah-Saravanan's scheme, Gope-Hwang's scheme and Islam et al's. scheme and last section provides the problem statement of our thesis.

Chapter 3

Proposed Scheme

The main problems with Karuppiah-Saravanan's scheme is that the Adversary $\mathcal{A}$ may easily impersonate the conversation, may perform replay attacks actively and passively and some secret parameters can be guessed easily, Gope-Hwang's scheme invites replay, DoS attacks and also unfair local verification of user and main flaws with Islam et al.'s scheme are that mutual authentication and user anonymity are not provided by Islam et al.'s scheme. Our proposed scheme is based on elliptic curve cryptography(ECC) that is type of asymmetric or public key cryptography(PKC) and we use one way hashing to improve the security of our scheme our scheme resists against all possible attacks and problems that are faced in authentication process of global mobility networks detailed security analysis is given in section(6). Previous schemes were based on symmetric encryption/decryption and our proposed scheme used ECC to propose the solution. Furthermore, proposed scheme consists of four phases initialization phase, registration phase, login and authentication, password change phase. Detailed description of all phases is as following:

3.1 Initialization Phase

In initialization phase, all entities and participants agree on elliptic curve (EC) parameters that are known globally P, n, a, b, p and participant computes their secret keys with the help of different parameters used in EEC.

3.2 Registration Phase

In registration phase the mobile user Mb_u freely chooses an Identity ID_{mbu}, a password PW_{mbu} and a random number $r \in Z_n^*$(natural number) as shown in figure 5 Afterward the Mb_u computes $U = h(PW_{mbu}||r)$ and transmits a message M to HA to request for registration, whereas $M = \{ID_{mbu}, U\}$.

When the home agent HA receives the registration request message he/she selects a random number $m \in Z_n^*$ and computes the following:

$$B = (U \oplus h(ID_{mbu}||m)) \tag{3.1}$$

$$N_{mbu} = h(ID_{mbu}||ID_{HA}||R_T \oplus U) \tag{3.2}$$

Where R_t is the registration time, after that the home agent HA stores $\{B, N_{mbu}, m, U, h(.)\}$ in SC and afterward the smart card(SC) is issued to Mb_u through a reliable network channel. The mobile user Mb_u generates and store r in smart card's storage, r is freshly generated random number of Mb_u. Now $\{B, m, ID_{mbu}, U, r, h(.)\}$ are stored in SC database.

$\mathcal{M}b_u$		$\mathcal{H}A$
Choose ID_{mbu}, PW_{mbu} Generate $r \in Z_n^*$ Compute $U = h(PW_{mbu}\|\|r)$		
	$\xrightarrow[(Secure-Channel)]{M=\{ID_{mbu}, U\}}$	Generate $m \in Z_n^*$ Compute $B = (U \oplus h(ID_{mbu}\|\|m))$ $N_{mbu} = h(ID_{mbu}\|\|ID_{HA}\|\|R_T \oplus U)$ Store $\{B, N_{mbu}\}$ in SC
	$\xleftarrow[(Secure-Channel)]{\{SC\}}$	
Choose r Store $\{B, ID_{mbu}, U, r, h(.)\}$		

Figure 3.1: Proposed Registration phase

3.3 Login Phase

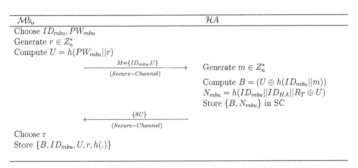

For authenticity we presume that recently, the Mobile user Mb_u is in foreign country under the administration of foreign network. The mobile user wants to use the mobile services in foreign area. To avail the mobile services in foreign region the mobile user firstly has to login with Identity and password and afterward for the security and legality he will authenticate himself/herself with the help of their foreign agent FA and home agent HA in a proper manner and will use the services with collaboration hosted country's network.

Step 1: $Mb_u \rightarrow FA : M1 = \{ID_{HA}, SID, V, Z, TS_{mbu}\}$

In first step the user Mb_u puts his card into the machine and uses his/her identity ID_{mbu} and password PW_{mbu} for login, on login request the machine calculates $B' = (U \oplus h(ID_{mbu}||m))$ that was saved at the registration phase and afterward Mb_u compares whether $B' \stackrel{?}{=} B$ if no then session is terminated and login request is rejected. If both B' and B are same then legality holds and The Smart card chooses random numbers $r_{mbu}, b \in Z_n^*$ and calculates the following:

$$Z = b.P \tag{3.3}$$

$$L = b.PK \tag{3.4}$$

$$K = h(N_{mbu} \oplus U) \tag{3.5}$$

$$SID = h(h(ID_{mbu}||R_T)||L) \tag{3.6}$$

$$V = h(K||SID||Z||TS_{mbu}) \tag{3.7}$$

Where, TS_{mbu} is timestamp of mobile user and P is a point over the elliptic-curve. Ultimately Mb_u sends login request message to foreign agent FA through an insecure channel.

3.4 Authentication Phase

Step 2: Our proposed scheme authenticates the user in four steps as shown in figure 2.3.4.3 and detailed explanation of our scheme is as followed:

$FA \rightarrow HA : M2 = \{M2 = \{M1, Y, C, TS_{FA}\}$ After receiving the message $M1$ foreign agent FA checks the time freshness TS_{mbu} if the comparison fails, FA does not accept the login request. Afterward Foreign agent checks $V' \stackrel{?}{=} V$ if yes then FA produces random number $r_{fa} \in Z_n^*$, and calculates the following:

$$V' \stackrel{?}{=} h(K||SID||Z||TS_{mbu}) \tag{3.8}$$

$$C = r_{fa}.P \tag{3.9}$$

$$Y = h(ID_{FA}||V'||FH_k||C||TS_{FA}) \tag{3.10}$$

Where, FH_k pre-shared key between foreign and home agent. After calculation of following values the foreign agent FA sends the M2 to home agent HA.

Step 3: $HA \rightarrow FA : M3 = \{D, K^*, V_1, K_0, V'', TS_{HA}\}$.

When HA receives the message $M2$, the Home agent HA confirms the whether the timestamp difference $TS_{HA} - TS_{FA} \leq \delta T$ if the verification fails, the Home agent does not accept the message $M2$. HA chooses random numbers $r_{ha}, d, e \in Z_n^*$ After that computes $Y^* = h(ID_{FA}||C||V'||Z||SID||TS_{FA}))$ and checks whether $Y^* \stackrel{?}{=} Y$ if true then HA proceeds to next step otherwise HA terminates the session. Then He/She verifies whether $V' \stackrel{?}{=} V$ if no then message is not accepted and session is terminated whereas, V'' is computed in eq.

$$Y^* = h(ID_{FA}||V'||FH_k||C||TS_{FA}) \tag{3.11}$$

$$Y^* \stackrel{?}{=} Y \tag{3.12}$$

$$V'' \stackrel{?}{=} h(K||SID||Z||TS_{mbu}) \tag{3.13}$$

$$D = cP \tag{3.14}$$

$$L = sZ \tag{3.15}$$

$$SID = h(h(ID_{mbu}||R_T)||L) \tag{3.16}$$

$$K^* = h(ID_{HA}||ID_{FA}||R_T) \tag{3.17}$$

$$SK = h(h(ID_{mbu}||K^*)||ID_{FA}||C||D) \tag{3.18}$$

$$K_0 = (SK \oplus (K^*||D||V'')) \tag{3.19}$$

$$V_1 = h(K^*||D||TS_{HA}) \tag{3.20}$$

$$\tag{3.21}$$

when the Home agent verifies all step then $M3 = \{D, K^*, V_1, K_0, V'', TS_{HA}\}$ is sent to Foreign agent FA for further authentication.

Step 4: $FA \rightarrow Mb_u : M4 = \{C', D, K^*, V_1, TS_{HA}, TS_{FA}\}$

When FA receives the $M3$, compares the timestamp freshness $TS_{mbu} - TS_{FA} \leq \delta T$ if comparison fails then FA does not accept the message. FA generates fresh $r'_f a$ calculates the following:

$$SK = (K_0 \oplus (K^*||D||V') \tag{3.22}$$

$$= SK \oplus (K^*||D||V') \oplus (K^*||D||V')$$

$$= \text{SK}$$

$C' = r'_{fa}P$ After the computation of session key at foreign agent side, the message $M4 = \{C', D, K^*, V_1, TS_{HA}, TS_{FA}\}$ is sent to mobile user Mb_u for further processing. On message M4 The mobile user Mb_u first of all checks the freshness of timestamp if timestamp is valid then checks $V_1' \stackrel{?}{=} h(K^*||D||TS_{HA})$ if result is false then session is terminated and if true then Mb_u is authenticated by foreign agent FA and home agent HA afterward Mb_u computes the session key that would share for further communication whereas, the session key is as following in eq.:

$$SK = h(h(ID_{mbu}||K)||ID_{FA}||C'||D) \tag{3.23}$$

3.5 Password change Phase

To enhance the security the proposed scheme allows the user to update or change their password. Whenever the mobile user Mb_u requests to change the password he/she has to perform the following steps:

Step 1: When a mobile user Mb_u with a smart card wants to change the password, he/she may change or update it. The mobile user has to login with his/her identity ID'_{mbu} and enters the password PW'_{mbu}.

Step 2: On the request the smartcard(SC) executes and verifies the following steps:

$$U^* = h(PW'_{mbu}||r) \tag{3.24}$$

After the calculation of U^* smart card checks whether $U^* \stackrel{?}{=} U$. If the values of U^* and U are not same then SC reject the request and if values are same then SC ensures the identity, password are legal and smart card requests the user to enter the new password PW_{mnew} that wants to keep where, PW_{mnew} is the new password.

Step 3: The Smart card calculate the following:

$$B^* = (U^* \oplus h(PW^*_{mnew}||m)) \tag{3.25}$$

$N^*_{mbu} = h(ID_{mbu}||ID_{HA}||R_T \oplus U^*)$ where, $\{B, U, N_{mbu}\}$ are replaced with $\{B^*, U^*, N^*_{mbu}\}$ and smart card carries $\{B^*, U^*, ID'_{mbu}, N^*_{mbu}, m, r, h(.)\}$.

$\mathcal{M}b_u$	$\mathcal{F}A$	$\mathcal{H}A$
Use ID_{mbu}, PW_{mbu} Verify $B' \stackrel{?}{=} (U \oplus h(ID_{mbu}\|\|m))$ Generate $b \in Z_n^*$ $Z = bP$ $L = bPK$ $K = h(N_{mbu} \oplus U)$ $SID = h(h(ID_{mbu}\|\|R_T)\|\|L)$ $V = h(K\|\|SID\|\|Z\|\|TS_{mbu})$		
$M1=\{ID_{HA},SID,V,Z,TS_{mbu}\}$ →		
	Check freshness TS_{mbu} Select $r_{fa} \in Z_n^*$ Verify $V' \stackrel{?}{=} h(K\|\|SID\|\|Z\|\|TS_{mbu})$ $C = r_{fa}.P$ $Y = h(ID_{FA}\|\|V'\|\|FH_k\|\|C\|\|TS_{FA})$	
	$M2=\{M1,Y,C,TS_{FA}\}$ →	
		$TS_{HA} - TS_{FA} \leq \delta T$ $Y^* = h(ID_{FA}\|\|V'\|\|FH_k\|\|C\|\|TS_{FA})$ verify $Y^* \stackrel{?}{=} Y$ $V'' \stackrel{?}{=} h(K\|\|SID\|\|L\|\|TS_{mbu})$ Choose $c \in Z_n^*$ $D = c.P$ $L = sZ$ $SID = h(h(ID_{mbu}\|\|R_T)\|\|L)$ $K^* = h(ID_{HA}\|\|ID_{FA}\|\|R_T)$ $SK =$ $h(h(ID_{mbu}\|\|K^*)\|\|ID_{FA}\|\|C\|\|D)$ $K_0 = (SK \oplus (K^*\|\|D\|\|V''))$ $V_1 = h(K^*\|\|D\|\|TS_{HA})$
		← $M3=\{D,K^*,V_1,K_0,V'',TS_{HA}\}$
	$TS_{FA} - TS_{HA} \leq \delta T$ $SK = (K_0 \oplus (K^*\|\|D\|\|V'')$ $C' = r'_{fa}P$	
	← $M4=\{C',D,K^*,V_1,TS_{HA},TS_{FA}\}$	
$TS_{mbu} - TS_{FA} \leq \delta T$ $V_1' = h(K^*\|\|D\|\|TS_{HA})$ check $V_1' \stackrel{?}{=} V_1$ $SK =$ $h(h(ID_{mbu}\|\|K)\|\|ID_{FA}\|\|C'\|\|D)$		

Figure 3.2: Proposed Scheme

3.6 Chapter Summary

This chapter of our thesis provides the proposed solution and its all steps(registration phase, login and authentication phase, password change phase) in detail.

Chapter 4

Security Analysis and Computation Cost Analysis

This chapter provides the security analysis and computation cost analysis of proposed thesis The detailed analysis is given in following sections:

4.1 Security Analysis

Security analysis of proposed scheme is done formally and informally. Formal analysis is done with BAN logic and proVerif, the informal analysis is checked against different attacks. Furthermore this section also shows the security requirement comparison.

4.1.1 Security Analysis with BAN logic

In this section we have provided the authentication proof of our scheme with BAN logic Burrows Abadi Needham(BAN) logic is based on some rules and the rules are used to determine the security of protocol [22][23]. The assumptions, idealized form and detailed proofs are discussed below: The Goals that are based on BAN logic of proposed scheme are discussed as follows:

- Goal 1: $FA| \equiv Mb_u \overset{SK}{\longleftrightarrow}$ FA
- Goal 2: $FA| \equiv Mb_u | \equiv Mb_u \overset{SK}{\longleftrightarrow}$ FA
- Goal 3: $HA| \equiv FA \overset{SK}{\longleftrightarrow}$ HA

Table 4.1: Notations

Notations	Description
$P\|\equiv X$	P believes X
$P \triangleleft X$	P sees X
$P\|\sim X$	P said X once
$P \Rightarrow X$	P has jurisdiction on X
$\#(X)$	X is fresh
(X,Y)	X, Y is part of formula(X,Y)
$< X >_Y$	X is combined with Y
$(X)_K$	Hash of message X with a key K
$P\xleftrightarrow{K}Q$	P and Q are using shared key K for communication
SK	Session key Sk is used in current section
$\frac{P\|\equiv P\xleftrightarrow{K}Q.p\triangleleft<X>_K}{P\|\equiv Q\|\sim X}$	Message-Meaning rule
$\frac{P\|\equiv\#(X)}{P\|\equiv\#(X,Y)}$	Freshness-conjuncatenation rule
$\frac{P\|\equiv\#(X),P\|\equiv Q\|\sim X}{P\|\equiv Q\|\equiv X}$	Nonce-verification rule
$\frac{P\|\equiv Q\Rightarrow X,P\|\equiv Q\|\equiv X}{P\|\equiv X}$	Jurisdiction rule

- Goal 4: $HA|\equiv FA|\equiv FA\xleftrightarrow{SK}$ HA
- Goal 5: $FA|\equiv HA\xleftrightarrow{SK}$ FA
- Goal 6: $FA|\equiv HA|\equiv HA\xleftrightarrow{SK}$ FA
- Goal 7: $Mb_u|\equiv FA\xleftrightarrow{SK}Mb_u$
- Goal 8: $Mb_u|\equiv FA|\equiv FA\xleftrightarrow{SK}Mb_u$

Part1: Idealized form of proposed protocol is given below:

- M1: Mb_u →FA: ID_{HA}, SID,$V :< Z >_K, TS_{mbu}$
- M2: FA →HA: M1,$Y :< C >_{FH_k}, TS_{FA}$
- M3: HA →FA: S,$V1 < D >_k^*, K_0 :< D >_k^*, TS_{FA}$
- M4: $FA \rightarrow Mb_u : V1, C' = r_f a.p, TS_{FA}$

Part2: Assumptions that are made to analyze the protocol are given below:

- A1: $Mb_u|\equiv \#(Z)$
- A2: $FA|\equiv \#(C), FA|\equiv \#(C')$
- A3: $HA|\equiv \#(D)(F)$
- A4: $Mb_u|\equiv Mb_u\xleftrightarrow{K}$ FA

- A5: $FA|\equiv FA\overset{FH_K}{\longleftrightarrow}$ HA
- A6: $HA|\equiv HA\overset{K^*}{\longleftrightarrow}$ FA
- A7: $FA|\equiv FA\overset{C'}{\longleftrightarrow}Mb_u$
- A8: $FA|\equiv Mb_u \Rightarrow Z$
- A9: $HA|\equiv Mb_u \Rightarrow Z$
- A10: $HA|\equiv FA \Rightarrow C$
- A11: $FA|\equiv HA \Rightarrow D$
- A12: $Mb_u|\equiv FA \Rightarrow C'$
- A13: $Mb_u|\equiv HA \Rightarrow D$

Part 3: Analysis of Idealized form of protocol that is derived on BAN logic assumptions and rules are stated as follows:
M1: Mb_u →FA: ID_{HA}, SID,$V :< Z >_K, TS_{mbu}$, TS_{mbu} is timestamp of Mb_u
By using seeing rule, we attain

- S1: $FA \lhd ID_{HA}, SID, V :< Z >_K, TS_{mbu}$

By using message-meaning rule and S1, we attain

- S2: $FA|\equiv Mb_u|\sim Z$

By using Freshness-conjuncatenation rule and S2, we attain

- S3: $FA|\equiv Mb_u|\equiv Z$

By using jurisdiction rule and S3, we attain

- S4:$FA|\equiv Z$

By using S4 and session key rule, we attain

- S5: $FA|\equiv Mb_u\overset{SK}{\longleftrightarrow}$ FA **(Goal 1)**

By using nonce-verification rule, we attain

- S6: $FA|\equiv Mb_u|\equiv Mb_u\overset{SK}{\longleftrightarrow}$ FA **(Goal 2)**

M2: $FA \rightarrow HA : M1, Y :< C >_{FHk}, TS_{FA}$. Where, TS_{FA} is timestamp of FA
By using the seeing rule, we attain

- S7: $HA \lhd M1, Y :< C >_F H_k, TS_{FA}$

By using message-meaning rule and S7, we attain

- S8: $HA|\equiv FA|\sim C$

By using Freshness-conjuncatenation rule and S8, we attain

- S9: $HA|\equiv Mb_u|\equiv C$

By applying the jurisdiction rule and S9, we attain

- S10:$HA|\equiv C$

By using the SK rule, we attain

- S11: $HA|\equiv FA\overset{SK}{\longleftrightarrow}$ HA **(Goal 3)**

Using nonce-verification rule and S11, we attain

- S12: $HA|\equiv FA|\equiv FA\overset{SK}{\longleftrightarrow}$ HA. **(Goal 4)**

M3: $HA \rightarrow$FA: S,$V1 < D >_k^*, K0 :< D >_k^*, TS_{FA}$,$TS_{HA}$ is timestamp of HA
By using the seeing-rule, we attain

- S13: $FA \triangleleft S, V1 < D >_k^*, K0 :< D >_k^*, TS_{FA}$

By using message-meaning rule and S13, we attain

- S14: $FA|\equiv HA|\sim D$

By using S14 the Freshness-conjuncatenation rule, we attain

- S15: $FA|\equiv HA|\equiv D$

By using the assumption A11,S15 and jurisdiction rule, we attain

- S16:$FA|\equiv D$

By using S4 and session-key rule, we attain

- S17: $FA|\equiv HA\overset{SK}{\longleftrightarrow}$ FA. **(Goal 5)**

And applying nonce-verification rule, we attain

- S18: $FA|\equiv HA|\equiv HA\overset{SK}{\longleftrightarrow}$ FA. **(Goal 6)**

M4: $FA \rightarrow Mb_u : V1, C' = r_f a.p, TS_{FA}$, TS_{FA} is timestamp of FA
By using the seeing rule, we attain

- S19: $Mb_u \triangleleft V1, C' = r_f a.p, TS_{FA}$

By using message-meaning rule and S19, we attain

- S20: $Mb_u|\equiv FA|\sim C'$

By using S20 and Freshness-conjuncatenation rule, we attain

- S21: $Mb_u|\equiv FA|\equiv C'$

By using the jurisdiction rule and S21, we attain

- S22: $Mb_u|\equiv C'$

By using session-key rule, we attain

- S23: $Mb_u|\equiv FA\overset{SK}{\longleftrightarrow}Mb_u$ **(Goal 7)**

And using nonce-verification rule, we attain

- S24: $Mb_u|\equiv FA|\equiv FA\overset{SK}{\longleftrightarrow}Mb_u$ **(Goal 8)**

By using the BAN logic we have shown that Mb_U, FA and HA achieved the mutual authentication and securely attain the session key agreement.

4.1.2 Security Analysis with ProVerif

We have verified the robustness and correctness of proposed scheme with ProVerif [?]. The ProVerif is automated reasoning software tool and ProVerif can test authentication, anonymity, reachable and all other security requirements[24]. ProVerif can support different cryptographic functions like: Encryption/decryption, MAC, signatures, hash, ecc and many others. [21],[25] In our proposed scheme we have used two types of channels ChSec:private and Chpub: public whereas, ChSec is secure channel and Chpub is a public or insecure channel. We have established secure channel between Mb_u and HA in registration phase and insecure channel between Mb_u, HA and FA in login phase and also in authentication phase. ID_{mbu} is real identity of Mb_u, ID_{HA} identity of HA and ID_{FA} identity of FA, SID is shadow identity TS is the timestamp and FH_k is key that is pre-shared between home agent HA and FA. All three participants compute session key SK. The ProVerif code correctness results are shown below. We used two channels one channel "ChSec" which is secure and "ChPub" is insure. We have used some constants P, Pk and s where, P is ECC point, PK is HA's public key and s is HA's secret key which is defined as private. We have declared h, XOR, Concat, Inverse, ECPA(Point-addition) and ECPME(Point-multiplication) as constructors

```
(* --------- Channels ----------*)
```

```
free ChSec:channel [private].  (*secure channel between Mbu and HA*)
free ChPub:channel.  (*public channel between Mbu,FA and HA*)
(*----------- Constants and Variables ---------*)
const P :bitstring.
Const PK: bitstring.
Const s: bitstring [private].
free FHk :bitstring [private].
free IDmbu :bitstring.
free IDFA :bitstring.
free IDHA :bitstring.
free PWmbu : bitstring [private].
(*========Constructors=======*)
fun h(bitstring):bitstring.
fun Inverse(bitstring):bitstring.
fun Concat(bitstring,bitstring):bitstring.
fun XOR(bitstring,bitstring):bitstring.
fun Mult(bitstring,bitstring):bitstring.
fun ECPM(bitstring,bitstring):bitstring.
fun ECPA(bitstring,bitstring):bitstring.
(*======Equations=======*)
equation forall a:bitstring; Inverse(Inverse(a))=a.
equation forall a:bitstring, b:bitstring; XOR(XOR(a,b),b)=a.
```

In Mbuprocess the Mb_u starts with registration phase, selects random number r, computes U and forwards (ID_{mbu}, U) to HA. Afterward Mb_u receives B and N_{mbu} from HA. In login phase Mb_u verifies B and after that chooses a random number b and computes SID,K, L, Z and V afterward he/she transmits $out(ChPub, (x_SID, xV, IDHA, Z, TSmbu))$ over public-channel. Mbu receives "in (ChPub,(xV1:bitstring,xC':bitstring,xTSFA:bitstring));" and verifies xV1' in case of true result the Mb_u calculates the session key with his/her K. FA and HA also performs same processes, with different parameters and values as defined below.

```
(*---------------Mobile User---------------------*)
(*=====*registration*======*)
let  pMbu=
(* Registration *)

new r :bitstring;
```

```
let U= h(Concat(PWmbu,r)) in
out (ChSec,(IDmbu,U));
in (ChSec,(B:bitstring,Nmbu:bitstring));
(*-------------Mbu login--------------*)
event start_Mbu(IDmbu);
new m :bitstring;
if (B=XOR(U,(h(Concat(IDmbu,m))))) then
new b :bitstring;
new TSFA :bitstring;
new TSHA: bitstring;
new TR :bitstring;
let Z = ECPM(b,P) in
let L = Mult(b,PK) in
let K =h(XOR(Nmbu,U)) in
let SID = h(h(Concat(IDmbu,(TR,L)))) in
new TSmbu :bitstring;
let xV = Concat(K,(SID,Z,TSmbu)) in
out(ChPub,(SID,xV,IDHA,Z,TSmbu));
in (ChPub,(xC':bitstring,xD:bitstring,xKstr:bitstring,V1:bitstring,xxTSFA:bitstring,xxTSHA:bitstring));
let xSK= h(h(Concat(IDmbu,(K,IDFA,TSHA)))) in
event end_Mbu(IDmbu)
else  0.

(*--------------------Foreign Agent---------------------*)
let pFA=
event start_FA(IDFA);
in(ChPub,(SID:bitstring,V:bitstring,xIDHA:bitstring,
Z:bitstring,TSmbu:bitstring));
new rfa : bitstring;
new TSFA :bitstring;
let C= ECPM(rfa,P) in
let Y= h(Concat(IDFA,(C,FHk,Z,SID,TSFA))) in
out(ChPub,((SID,V,IDHA,Z,TSmbu),Y,C,TSFA));
in (ChPub,(xD:bitstring,V1:bitstring,xK0:bitstring,xKstr:bitstring,xV'':bitstring,xTSHA:bitstring));
let C'=ECPM(rfa,P)in
out(ChPub,(C',Kstr,V1,TSHA,TSFA));
event end_FA(IDFA)
```

```
else  0.

(*=====*reg*======*)
(*------------------------------Home Agent------------------------*)
let pHA=
(*---- Registration ----*)
in (ChSec,(xIDmbu:bitstring,U:bitstring));
new m:bitstring;
let B = XOR(U,Concat(IDmbu,m))in
let Nmbu =XOR(h(Concat(IDmbu,IDHA)),U) in
out(ChSec, (B,Nmbu));
(*-----------------Authentication-process-----------------*)
in (ChPub,(M1:bitstring,Y:bitstring,C':bitstring,TSFA:bitstring));
event start_HA(IDHA);
new C: bitstring;
new e: bitstring;
new Z: bitstring;
new TSHA: bitstring;
new c: bitstring;
new TSmbu: bitstring;
new TR: bitstring;
let D = ECPM(c,P) in
let F = ECPM(e,P) in
let L = Mult(s,Z) in
let x_SID = h(h(Concat(IDmbu,(TR,L)))) in
let Kstar= h(Concat(IDFA,(IDHA,TR,F))) in
let xSK = h(h(Concat(IDmbu,(Kstar,IDFA,C',D,TSHA)))) in
let K0 = XOR(SK,h(Concat(Kstar,D))) in
let V1 =  h(Concat(Kstar,(D,TSHA))) in
out (ChPub,(D,Kstr,V1,K0,V'',TSHA));
event end_HA(IDHA)
else
0.
```

The parallel execution of all processes of proposed protocol is shown below:

```
process ((!pMbu) | (!pFA) | (!pHA) )
```

With the following queries the authentication property is verified:

```
(*-------queries------*)
free SK:bitstring [private].
query attacker(SK).
query id:bitstring; inj-event(end_Mbu(IDmbu)) ==> inj-event(start_Mbu(IDmbu)).
query id:bitstring; inj-event(end_FA(IDFA)) ==> inj-event(start_FA(id)).
query id:bitstring; inj-event(end_HA(id)) ==> inj-event(start_HA(id)).
```

Six events are used in proposed code Mb_u's events(begin/end), FA events(begin/end) and HA's events(begin/end).

```
(*=====*Events*=====*)
event start_Mbu(bitstring).
event end_Mbu(bitstring).
event start_FA(bitstring).
event end_FA(bitstring).
event start_HA(bitstring).
event end_HA(bitstring).
```

The results are shown below:

```
1-- Query inj-event(end_HA(id)) ==> inj-event(start_HA(id))
Completing...
Starting query inj-event(end_HA(id)) ==> inj-event(start_HA(id))
RESULT inj-event(end_HA(id)) ==> inj-event(start_HA(id)) is true.
2--Query inj-event(end_FA(IDFA[])) ==> inj-event(start_FA(id_1281))
Completing...
Starting query inj-event(end_FA(IDFA[])) ==> inj-event(start_FA(id_1281))
RESULT inj-event(end_FA(IDFA[])) ==> inj-event(start_FA(id_1281)) is true.
3-- Query inj-event(end_Mbu(IDmbu[])) ==> inj-event(start_Mbu(IDmbu[]))
Completing...
Starting query inj-event(end_Mbu(IDmbu[])) ==> inj-event(start_Mbu(IDmbu[]))
RESULT inj-event(end_Mbu(IDmbu[])) ==> inj-event(start_Mbu(IDmbu[])) is true.
4-- Query not attacker(SK[])
Completing...
Starting query not attacker(SK[])
RESULT not attacker(SK[]) is true.
```

Result 1,2 and 3 are showing that all three processes are successfully started and terminated.

Whereas, result 4 shows that the adversary cannot find the session key SK. Hence proposed scheme preserves the secrecy and authentication.

4.1.3 Informal Security Analysis

Our proposed scheme accomplishes all possible security risks as stated below:

1. User anonymity.
2. User untraceability.
3. Man-in-Middle attack.
4. Backward/Forward secrecy.
5. Replay attacks.
6. Known-key attacks.
7. User friendliness.
8. Local User and Password verification.
9. Insider attacks.
10. Stolen- verifier attacks.
11. Mutual authentication.
12. Impersonation attacks(Forgery attacks)
13. Dos attacks.

4.1.3.1 User Anonymity

User anonymity is considered an important factor while designing a secure scheme, a user identity should not revealed to anyone except the legal claimed user. A secure protocol protects personal data and sensitive information of a user so, an attacker/adversary could not analyze any information that can help to breach the security requirements.
Proposed Scheme achieves the anonymity requirements because we used strong encryptions techniques in our proposed scheme we used hash function in registration phase, $M = \{ID_{mbu}, U\}$ is sent through secure and reliable channel and we used random numbers that protects our messages.

In login-authentication phase lets suppose adversary A captures the message $M1 = \{SID, V, ID_{HA}$ $, Z, TS_{mbu}\}$ and tires to attain the ID_{mbu} but, identity of mobile user is saved in SID and $SID = (ID_{mbu}||Z||R_T||L)$ is concatenated with L, Adversary A cannot extract SID because L cannot be obtained neither in SC nor L is sent through any message so, we can say that our proposed scheme achieves all requirements of user anonymity.

4.1.3.2 User Untraceability

For a secure protocol user traceability is vulnerable issue because, a legal user traceability may leads to many attacks. Our scheme does not disclose login information or previous history because we used random numbers($r_{ha}, r_{fa}, r_{mbu}, b, c, d$) with elliptic-curve points P, it is impossible for an attacker to guess random number. Hence in our scheme mobile user Mb_u is untraceable.

4.1.3.3 Man-in-Middle attack

A type of security attack in which a malicious adversary or attacker illicitly inserts Himself/herself in a two parties communication and intercepts their conversation. The Adversary can capture the sensitive data/information, can send or receive data anytime and may impersonate both parties by pretending Himself/Herself a legal user.

In our proposed scheme adversary or attacker cannot perform the Man-In-Middle attack because our proposed scheme provides mutual authentication and endpoint authentication at each side. In our proposed scheme we used the timestamps of each participant with every message $\{M1, M2, M3, M4\}$ first of all time difference is checked at each end if time difference is valid then session begins else more we used ellpitic-cureve points P with each random number so adversary cannot guess any secret or public key nor the adversary can compute the session key in addition our SK establishment is fully fair. Hence, Our proposed scheme can prevents the Man-In-Middle attacks.

4.1.3.4 Backward/Forward secrecy

Backward secrecy is a type of secrecy in which if an adversary A if aware of new session key he/she would be unable to obtain the the earlier keys. While the forward secrecy means any compromization of old session key should not reveal any future keys for the adversary A.

Our proposed scheme fulfills all forward-backward secrecy requirements due to random numbers because, with a new session random numbers are chosen newly even if L is compromised at any stage later still, may not compute the SK. Therefore we can say that our proposed-scheme accomplishes backward/forward secrecy.

4.1.3.5 Replay Attacks

In replay attacks the malicious attacker/adversary repeats or delays the transmission. There are three participants in Global-Mobility-Networks $Mb_u, FAandHA$ who authenticate each other and four messages are transmitted among them $\{M1, M2, M3, M4\}$ over a public channel. Lets assume an adversary A captures the $M1 = \{SID, V, ID_{HA}, Z, TS_{mbu}\}$ and tries to perform the replay attack to FA. On $M1$ FA compares the timestamps if it is valid then message is accepted otherwise message would be rejected by FA if adversary generates a timestamps TS'_{mbu} and timestamp comparison becomes true then adversary tries to compute V' which is impossible for adversary because adversary has no knowledge of values saved in V' so adversary cannot forge FA. Similarly we used timestamps with all messages M2,M3,M4 and TS comparison at each session also some other comparisons of different values at different sessions so, an adversary cannot replay any message. Further, without knowing ID_{mbu} the adversary is unable to compute the Sk and we have encrypted ID_{mbu} with L which in unguessable for an attacker. Due to following reasons, our proposed-scheme can resist the replay attacks.

4.1.3.6 Known-key attacks

Known-key-attack is cryptographic attack in which an attacker/adversary can access the ciphertext. Known-key-attacks are possibly attempted successfully by an attacker/adversary when palintext is associated with ciphertext and adversary could trace plaintext by just performing backtracking.
In our proposed scheme as stated in section 7.2, 7.3 we used the elliptic-curve points with different random numbers for all sessions when session ends random numbers are freshly generated. Furthermore our session key is created with all three participants at each end independently. If attacker gets the previous session key He/She cannot compute new session key and if he/she gets the new session key still may not compute the previous one because of ECC-points, random numbers and timestampts. Proposed scheme resist the known-key-attacks.

4.1.3.7 User Friendliness

A secure and useful protocol fulfills all requirements of a user friendly scheme, in which a user is allowed to select his/her identity ID_{mbu} and password PW_{mbu} freely and provides freedom to change our update his/her password to enhance the security and etc.
Proposed scheme permits the users to select an identity ID_{mbu} and password PW_{mbu} freely with their choice whereas, the SC verifies the inputs and correctness. User may freely chooses the random number and also can change or updates his/her password so password may keep save from attackers and adversaries.

4.1.3.8 Local User and Password verification

To avoid the illegal access our scheme provide the password verification in registration phase also in login-authentication phase, in registration phase the mobile user Mb_u computed $U = (PW_{mbu}||r)$ and then computes $B = (U \oplus h(ID_{mbu}||m))$ where, in login-authentication phase is re-verified locally if $B' \stackrel{?}{=} B$ then the login phase proceeds to next step otherwise session in aborted. So, by using local password-verification we enhanced our proposed scheme more secure.

4.1.3.9 Insider attacks

Insider attack may defined as malicious network attack that is committed by an authorized person with legal access. In our proposed scheme let's suppose some insider of home agent HA tries to attain the password of mobile user Mb_u, the mobile user Mb_u transmits $M = \{ID_{mbu}, U\}$ on secure channel/network. The HA's insider can get the message but could not compute the U because $U = h(PW_{mbu}||r)$ to extract the U and one-way-hash insider must have to known the random number and r as we know that it is infeasible for an insider attacker to compute the hash and r. So, by following assumptions we say that our scheme may prevents the insider attacks.

4.1.3.10 Stolen- verifier attacks

Proposed scheme resist the stolen-verifier-attacks because the verification of password tables are stored at mobile user Mb_u side nor the HA and FA's can get any information about the password. If SC is stolen then no one can extract the password because password is save in U and we have taken the hash function so. adversary cannot alter the password. Hence, proposed scheme can resist the stolen-verifier attacks.

4.1.3.11 Mutual authentication

Mutual authentication is feature of security in which all participants of a protocol mutually authenticates each other at same time. Our scheme achieves all conditions of mutual authentication furthermore our scheme furnished mutual authentication between all three participants Mb_u, FA and HA.

4.1.3.11.1 Mb_u and HA Mutual authentication In our scheme Mb_u authenticates the HA by verifying the $V_1' \stackrel{?}{=} V_1$ in step 4 and HA confirms the Mb_u by checking $V'' \stackrel{?}{=} h(K||SID||L||TS_{mbu})$ in step 2 only a legitimate user can compute V_1' and V'' where both participants transfers the secret parameter ID_{mbu} with each other also both participants computes the SK mutually so Mb_u and FA authenticates each other mutually in proposed scheme.

4.1.3.11.2 HA and FA Mutual authentication Likewise FA and HA authenticates each other in step 3 HA verifies $Y^* \stackrel{?}{=} h(ID_{FA}||V'||FH_k||C||TS_{FA})$ where Y is computed by real foreign agent FA because preshared key FH_k is used in Y so, in step 3 FA is authenticated by HA. Whereas, in step 4FA verifies $S' \stackrel{?}{=} (SK||ID_{FA}||C||TS_{mbu})F$ and S is computed by legal HA because of SK after the authentication of HA by FA SK is computed here mutually so, our scheme provides the mutual authenticity of FA and HA. .

4.1.3.11.3 FA and Mbu Mutual authentication FA authenticates Mb_u in step 1 by checking $V' \stackrel{?}{=} h(K||SID||Z||TS_{mbu})$ there is $Mb_u's$ timestamp and only a legal Mb_u can compute V. So, after the verification of $V' \stackrel{?}{=} V$ the foreign agent FA authenticates Mb_u.

4.1.3.12 Impersonation attacks

Impersonation attack means an adversary may forge a legitimate user by pretending himself/herself a legal user. Adversary/attacker can delete or modify any message in different manners or can forge the other participants of a communication channel. In proposed scheme we withstand the forgery attacks in following ways as stated below:

4.1.3.12.1 Mb_uImpersonation attacks

Suppose the adversary A has intercepted the login message $M1 = \{SID, V, ID_{HA}, Z, TS_{mbu}\}$ in step 1 whereas, the message M1 was sent by legal Mb_u to FA in past session and the adversary will try to forge Mb_u. The Adversary A will send login message M1 to FA. FA receives the M1 and verifies the timestamp and its freshness here the comparison fails and login request will not be accepted by FA. Now the adversary will generate a new timestamp $\overline{TS_{mbu}}$ and will resend $M1 = \{SID, V, ID_{HA}, Z, \overline{TS_{mbu}}\}$ to FA. FA Checks the TS_{mbu} and comparison will successful afterward FA checks whether $V' \stackrel{?}{=} h(K||SID||Z||TS_{mbu})$ whereas V is not equal to V' so request is rejected. Adversary may also try to impersonate in step 4 but due to comparison of V1' with V1 the adversary will fail to play the impersonation game in each phase.

4.1.3.12.2 FA Impersonation attacks

In step 2 adversary will try to impersonate the HA by sending message $M2 = \{M1, Y, C, TS_{FA}\}$. Without knowing the preshared key FH_k the adversary cannot impersonate the FA. Furthermore our scheme provides the comparison $Y^* \stackrel{?}{=} h(ID_{FA}||V'||FH_k||C||TS_{FA})$ at step 2. In case of any wrong value the message will be rejected. Furthermore HA and FA shares the SK and without the knowledge of SK the adversary is unable to impersonate the message $M4 = \{V_1, C', TS_{FA}\}$. Thus our scheme can easily resist the impersonation attacks.

4.1.3.12.3 HA Impersonation attacks

In step 3 the adversary will try to forge the message $M3 = \{S, V_1, k_0, TS_{HA}$ but first check the timestamp difference $TS_{FA} - TS_{HA} \leq \delta T$ here the δT becomes false so message will not be accepted suppose the timestamp difference becomes true with adversary's Timestamp $\overline{TS_{HA}}$. Still our protocol checks whether $S' \stackrel{?}{=} (SK||ID_{FA}||C||TS_{mbu})F$ adversary cannot compute S' so Adversary will fail to play the forgery. Thus we can say that our proposed protocol can easily resist the HA impersonation.

4.1.4 Security Requirements and Comparison

The main purpose of this section is to determine the analysis of security requirements and to find out the computation cost and performance analysis of our proposed scheme. The subsection elaborates security comparison and the cost comparison of proposed scheme with other related work.

4.1.5 Security Requirements

This section provides the comparison of security and cost requirements of our proposed scheme with the schemes which are proposed in following articles[8][14] [17] [18]. We compared all 13 security requirements of our proposed scheme with some previous work whereas, R is security requirement so R1 is requirement 1 and so on. The comparison table shows that only our scheme provides all 13 requirements. The detailed comparison is shown in table. The security analysis shows that only our proposed scheme can fulfill all security requirements.

4.2 Computation Cost Analysis

To measure the computation cost we ignore some lightweight function such as concatenations, XOR due to their limited computation cost. Our main attention is to analyze cryptographic operation that FA, Mb_u and HA need to execute. We consider all three participants FA, Mb_u and HA. Detailed description is shown in table.

In performance analysis section we compared our proposed scheme with few previous schemes. To evaluate the performance of our scheme we compared our proposed scheme with following schemes:[17], [18] and [19] these schemes are proposed recently. The total computation cost of scheme [17] is 17Th+2Tse+3Tme, total computation cost of scheme[18] is 14Th+2Tse+3Tmo+1TQr, total computation cost of scheme [19] is 11Th+6Tecmp+5Tecpa and the total computation cost of our proposed scheme is 11Th+6Tecmp+5Tecpa . The detailed description is illustrated in table 4.

- CC:Computation cost
- Th: CC of single hash function;
- Tme: CC of modular exponentiation;
- Tse: CC of symmetric encryption;
- Tsd: CC of symmetric decryption;
- Tecmp: CC of ECC point multiplication(PM);

Requirements	[18]	[17]	[14]	[11]	[8]	Proposed Scheme
R1	✓	✓	✓	×	×	✓
R2	✓	✓	✓	×	×	✓
R3	✓	✓	✓	✓	✓	✓
R4	✓	✓	✓	✓	✓	✓
R5	×	×	×	✓	✓	✓
R6	✓	×	✓	×	✓	✓
R7	✓	✓	✓	×	×	✓
R8	×	✓	×	×	✓	✓
R9	✓	✓	✓	×	✓	✓
R10	✓	✓	×	✓	✓	✓
R11	✓	✓	✓	✓	✓	✓
R12	×	×	✓	✓	✓	✓
R13	×	✓	✓	✓	✓	✓

Table 4.2: Security requirements table

- R1:User anonymity.
- R2:User untraceability.
- R3:Man-in-Middle attack.
- R4:Backward/Forward secrecy.
- R5:Replay attacks.
- R6:Known-key attacks.
- R7:User friendliness.
- R8:Local User and Password verification.
- R9:Insider attacks.
- R10:Stolen-verifier attacks.
- R11:Mutual authentication.
- R12:Impersonation attacks
- R13:Dos attacks.

✓: Yes provides, ×: Does not provide

Computation Cost	Karuppiah and Saravanan	Gope and Hwang	Islam et al.	Proposed Scheme
CC_{mbu}	6Th+1Tse+3Tme	5Th+1Tme	7Th+2Tme	6Th+2Tecmp+1Tecpa
CC_{HA}	8Th+1Tsd+1Tme	6Th+1Tsd+1TQr	5Th+2Tme	4Th+2Tecmp+3Tecpa
CC_{FA}	3Th	3Th+1Tse	4Th+2Tme	1Th+2Tecmp+1Tecpa
CC_{Total}	17Th+2Tse+3Tme	14Th+2Tse+3Tmo+1TQr	16Th+6Tme	11Th+6Tecmp+5Tecp

Table 4.3: Comparison of computation cost and running time

CC_{mbu}: Computation-cost of Mb_u
CC_{HA} : Computation-cost of FA
CC_{FA} : Computation-cost of HA
CC_{total} : Total computation-cost.

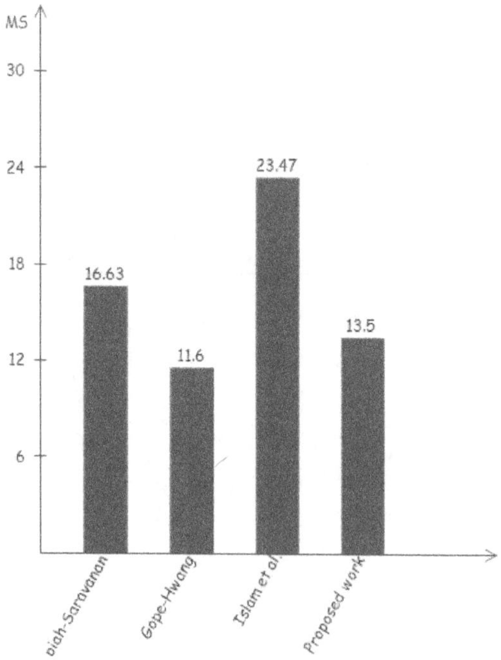

To measure the running time of our proposed solution we followed Kilinc and Yanik [26] experiments. Single Th takes 0.00023ms, Tecmp takes 2.226ms,Tecpa takes 0.0288ms,Tme takes 3.8500. We mentioned here the total running time of all proposed scheme, our proposed scheme takes total 13.624ms whereas [19] takes total 23.4680ms, [18] takes total proximately 11.5964ms and [17] takes total 16.6323ms. As a result, the running time of our Proposed scheme is very efficient as compared to schmes [17] and [19]. The scheme [18] has less running time as compared to our proposed scheme but the scheme [18] is vulnerable to numerous attacks and only our proposed scheme can resist all attacks as compared to previous schemes that are discussed in this section.

4.3 Chapter Summary

This chapter describes formal security analysis, informal security analysis, comparison of security requirements, computation costs and running time of our proposed scheme in detail.

Chapter 5

Conclusion and Future work

This thesis scrutinizes some recent authentication schemes in GLOMONET and discloses that these proposed (Karuppiah-Saravanan, Gope-Hwang, Islam et al.) schemes suffer with many security threat and challenges and cannot withstand various security attacks. Security weakness and cryptanalysis of following shemes are shown in chapter 2. Thus, this thesis proposed An Improved and Robust Anonymous Authentication Scheme for Roaming in GLOMONET to overcome these flaws. Formal verification with BAN logic and ProVerif have shown the correctness of proposed work. Informal security comparison shows that our scheme can resist different attacks and performance analysis shows that scheme has performed efficient performance as compared to previous work discussed in our thesis. In future work we will try to propose IBE schemes in which foreign agent will authenticate the Mobile user without connecting their Home Agent, the authentication procedure would be between mobile user and foreign agent.

Bibliography

[1] Zhu J, Ma J. A new authentication scheme with anonymity for wireless environments. *Consumer Electronics, IEEE Transactions on* 2004; **50**(1):231–235.

[2] Lee CC, Hwang MS, Liao IE. Security enhancement on a new authentication scheme with anonymity for wireless environments. *Industrial Electronics, IEEE Transactions on* 2006; **53**(5):1683–1687.

[3] Wei Y, Qiu H, Hu Y. Security analysis of authentication scheme with anonymity for wireless environments 2006; :1–4.

[4] Wu CC, Lee WB, Tsaur WJ, *et al.*. A secure authentication scheme with anonymity for wireless communications. *IEEE Communications Letters* 2008; **12**(10):722–723.

[5] Lee CH, Hwang MS, Yang WP. Enhanced privacy and authentication for the global system for mobile communications. *Wireless networks* 1999; **5**(4):231–243.

[6] Xu J, Feng D. Security flaws in authentication protocols with anonymity for wireless environments. *ETRI journal* 2009; **31**(4):460–462.

[7] He D, Ma M, Zhang Y, Chen C, Bu J. A strong user authentication scheme with smart cards for wireless communications. *Computer Communications* 2011; **34**(3):367–374.

[8] Li CT, Lee CC. A novel user authentication and privacy preserving scheme with smart cards for wireless communications. *Mathematical and Computer Modelling* 2012; **55**(1):35–44.

[9] Jeon W, Lee Y, Won D. An efficient user authentication scheme with smart cards for wireless communications. *International Journal of Security & Its Applications* 2013; **7**(4):1–5.

[10] Das AK. A secure and effective user authentication and privacy preserving protocol with smart cards for wireless communications. *Networking Science* 2013; **2**(1-2):12–27.

[11] Yoon EJ, Yoo KY, Ha KS. A user friendly authentication scheme with anonymity for wireless communications. *Computers & Electrical Engineering* 2011; **37**(3):356–364.

[12] Niu J, Li X. A novel user authentication scheme with anonymity for wireless communications. *Security and Communication Networks* 2014; **7**(10):1467–1476.

[13] Li CT. A more secure and efficient authentication scheme with roaming service and user anonymity for mobile communications. *Information Technology and Control* 2012; **41**(1):69–76.

[14] Jiang Q, Ma J, Li G, Yang L. An enhanced authentication scheme with privacy preservation for roaming service in global mobility networks. *Wireless Personal Communications* 2013; **68**(4):1477–1491.

[15] Wen F, Susilo W, Yang G. A secure and effective anonymous user authentication scheme for roaming service in global mobility networks. *Wireless personal communications* 2013; **73**(3):993–1004.

[16] Farash MS, Chaudhry SA, Heydari M, Sadough S, Mohammad S, Kumari S, Khan MK. A lightweight anonymous authentication scheme for consumer roaming in ubiquitous networks with provable security. *International Journal of Communication Systems* 2015; .

[17] Karuppiah M, Saravanan R. A secure authentication scheme with user anonymity for roaming service in global mobility networks. *Wireless Personal Communications* 2015; **84**(3):2055–2078.

[18] Gope P, Hwang T. Enhanced secure mutual authentication and key agreement scheme preserving user anonymity in global mobile networks. *Wireless Personal Communications* 2015; **82**(4):2231–2245.

[19] Islam SH, Khan MK, Obaidat MS, Muhaya FTB. Provably secure and anonymous password authentication protocol for roaming service in global mobility networks using extended chaotic maps. *Wireless Personal Communications* 2015; **84**(3):2013–2034.

[20] Xu J, Zhu WT, Feng DG. An improved smart card based password authentication scheme with provable security. *Computer Standards & Interfaces* 2009; **31**(4):723–728.

[21] Naqvi H, Chaudhry SA, Mahmood K. An improved authentication protocol for sip-based voip. 2016.

[22] Amin R, Biswas G. A secure light weight scheme for user authentication and key

agreement in multi-gateway based wireless sensor networks. *Ad Hoc Networks* 2016; **36**:58–80.

[23] Blanchet. This is a test test entry of type @MISC and 'howpublished'. http://www.prosecco.gforge.inria.fr/personal/bblanche/proverif/ Jun 1990.

[24] Burrows M, Abadi M, Needham RM. A logic of authentication. *Proceedings of the Royal Society of London A: Mathematical, Physical and Engineering Sciences*, vol. 426, The Royal Society, 1989; 233–271.

[25] Kilinc HH, Yanik T. A survey of sip authentication and key agreement schemes. *IEEE Communications Surveys & Tutorials* 2014; **16**(2):1005–1023.

[26] Zhang G, Fan D, Zhang Y, Li X, Liu X. A privacy preserving authentication scheme for roaming services in global mobility networks. *Security and Communication Networks* 2015; **8**(16):2850–2859.

www.ingramcontent.com/pod-product-compliance
Lightning Source LLC
La Vergne TN
LVHW052314060326
832902LV00021B/3881
* 9 7 8 3 9 6 0 6 7 1 4 7 3 *